HOW TO COME UP WITH GREAT IDEAS AND ACTUALLY MAKE THEM HAPPEN

EWAN McINTOSH

First published in 2014
by NoTosh Publishing

This edition published in 2015

Text copyright © 2014 Ewan McIntosh
Ewan McIntosh has asserted his right under the Copyright,
Designs and Patents Act 1988 to be identified as the author of
this work.

All rights reserved. No part of this publication may be
reproduced, stored in a retrieval system, or transmitted in any
form or by any means, electronic, mechanical, photocopying,
recording, or otherwise, without the prior permission of the
publisher.

A CIP catalogue record for this book is available from the
British Library

10 9 8 7 6 5 4 3 2 1

ISBN-13: 978-1-909779-04-4

NoTosh Publishing
a division of NoTosh Limited
27 Lauriston Street
Edinburgh EH3 9DQ

www.notosh.com

DEDICATION

I count on writing more than my first book, and so will save a dedication for Catriona (now 6) and Anna (now 3) as motivation to put pen to paper, finger to keyboard, before too long. But they deserve a thank you, too, for putting up with Daddy's squeaky door opening far too early in the morning for a bout of writing. Writing a book is tough, if you want to try to do it well. Sure, you don't have a 'boss' telling you what to write, how to write it, how to reference it or questioning, too much, the point of the stories you're telling. But you do have your own integrity on the line. That integrity, to myself and to the amazing team with whom I work (Tom, Peter, Hamish, David, Joanna, Rachel and Kieran) is more powerful for making one push beyond midnight to get the words down, the photographs chosen, the layout just the way you want it. But the price is all-too-often paid by one's family. For that, Morgane, I am eternally grateful, which is why my first book is dedicated, without hesitation, to you and you alone - the person who has perhaps offered the greatest sacrifices to get it off the presses, electronic and paper, in the first place.

Ewan McIntosh

This is a black and white, text only version of a book originally designed as a full colour, highly photographic guide.

You can buy this directly from:
www.notosh.com

CONTENTS

INTRODUCTION

Who needs an innovation strategy?	9
What this book is not	11
Balancing individual innovation with the team	13
Happy Learning	15
But we're doing so well…	19

MOVING BEYOND ISLANDS OF EXCELLENCE

The challenge of "one room innovation"	27
Joined up thinking	30
From Mystery to Algorithmic Innovation	35
The Three Horizons	39

THE FIRST HORIZON: ASSUME NOTHING

Setting up your collaborative team	46
Innovation under your nose	52
Immersion: Gathering the evidence	67

THE FIRST HORIZON: PROBLEM FINDING

Synthesis: Defining your pain	101
Recall and remember	104
Connect and cluster	106

Defining problems that haven't been solved	109

THE THIRD HORIZON: REACHING FOR THE STARS

What's your BHAG?	119
Big ideas in the small stuff	122
Crossing the chasm	125
Beyond pilots	133
Ideation: generating ideas	136
Ideation: refining ideas	162
Building better ideas through creative conflict	163

THE SECOND HORIZON

Prototyping culture	177
Explaining (and changing) your ideas	192
Actor mapping: strategy built around people	196
Pitching your idea	203

MOVING FROM CONCEPT TO DELIVERY

When is a prototype 'done'?	209
Rome wasn't built in a day, but 30 days would do	213
Don't think, try	218
REFERENCES	223

INTRODUCTION

'Innovation distinguishes between a leader and a follower.'
Steve Jobs

Ewan McIntosh

WHO NEEDS AN INNOVATION STRATEGY?

Is there a viable, repeatable process for innovation that helps the education world move beyond a reliance on individual talent doing wonders within the four walls of their classroom? Yes. That's what this book will share with you, through practical steps, workshop activities you can undertake with your own teams in your learning environment, and with plenty of stories of what success looks like.

What could schools ever learn from luxury fashion houses, political campaigners, global tech, media and telecommunications companies, and the world's biggest businesses of tomorrow, the startups? Each week, I get to work in both domains - schools and universities on the one hand, and creative organisations on the other - and there is much for each group to learn from the other when it comes to leading innovation.

In the time I spend with school leaders and teachers, I see many struggling with overload, rejection and abortive attempts at innovation. Why does the formal education sector seem to have so much pain in creating fast change, resistance to it even? And are the challenges faced in education any different to those faced by the fashion, media or telecoms companies?

Think of all those conference keynote speakers who have, since the turn into this twenty-first century, reminded audiences that doctors from the beginning of the twentieth century walking into surgery today wouldn't recognise their theatre, whereas teachers would be quite at home. They have a (partial) point. Change in the classroom is less visibly radical than one might see in many forms of industry, business and even Government.

In today's schools, what is it that really counts? What is it that we want to change so badly with our strategy documents and vision statements? There is a gulf between what schools say counts – increasing children's creativity, responsible citizenship, confident learners, workers and entrepreneurs-to-be – and what appears to count: passing the test or meeting the demands of today can end up taking all precedence in the end over what we could achieve tomorrow.

On this level, many argue that school these days is as industrial in its complex as it was 100 years ago. We ship them in, we fill them up, we send them out with grades. The more and the better the grades are, the more successful the system has been.

I don't believe for one minute that this is the reality in many schools, based on some of the amazingly innovative classrooms I'm lucky enough to work in. But there's a grain of truth in the general less-than-lightning pace of innovation in most formal education environments, compared to that which we see in the technology, media or fashion industries, for example.

If we know *how* we might move from the reality of the status quo to what we envision, then we can start to construct lessons, conversations with parents, curricula, school buildings and whole education systems that promote the educational values we all want, whether we're the young people going through the system, their parents, future employers or Government ministries seeking more entrepreneurs.

The *how*, not the *what*, is what we will explore here.

This book will help you achieve ambitious visions for learning through swift innovation. We will borrow from those paths of life where people invent what we all end up using tomorrow, create much from very little, and refine their ideas with a swiftness few of those in larger corporations, Government or schools are used to seeing.

The book is organised into three broad sections designed to lead you and your team through the key tactics, strategies and discussion points involved in identifying where potential for innovation in learning might lie, how we might frame our mission and how we get there.

You can also dip in and out when you are at a particular point in defining or making your great ideas happen. You can also use the resources at notosh.com/lab to support your efforts. Above all: have fun innovating!

WHAT THIS BOOK IS NOT

I've never been a fan of business ideas being imported lock, stock and barrel into the education space.

I can't think of one that has succeeded. British academic and agent provocateur Fred Garnett reflected back in 2010 on what he saw as an emerging use of 'business models' in the English education system being used as a way to edge out creativity, connectedness, collaboration and replace it with competition, metrification and accountability in the most top-down managerial kind of manner:

> *So why do we keep being offered a business model version of educational policy, rather than a learning process model such as "Learning is Delicious," especially in those circumstances when educational professionals offer a fresh, clear vision of learning. Critically the business model approach allows a number of things to be done to education that make sense from a central government perspective. Firstly it can be commoditised,*

productised, homogenised and advertised; EDUCATION! Then "leaders" can be found, trained, promoted, handcuffed, lionised, blamed and replaced.

I responded with what I see as the key difference between the failed attempts to bring traditional business models to education and the success we're seeing in bringing creative attitudes from creative startups to learning. There are a few interesting differences between these startups and the corporates that have already grown too big.

First – they're owned by a small team who understand from the get-go that they need to find, nurture and involve a community of users to help build and scale their idea quickly enough to succeed.

They're small enough to realise that many heads are cleverer than a couple, and they come up with ingenious ways to harness that.

Policymakers, on the other hand, are generally the equivalent of the publicly owned corporations that have always had and continue to have a great deal of trouble understanding this disruptive way of working. They are often the ones to ask incredulously 'Where's the business model?' because they're seeking their business mode, the one where they are in control.

As an investor I have always gone with the small guys and gals who understand that the people in the community around them are the principal 'owners' of the product or service – they have a better chance of success.

In education environments, it is no different. By moving innovation and change from the leadership suite to the students, parents and teachers in a community, and providing them with frameworks and toolsets to understand how to do this successfully, the benefits of all our ideas will be greatly enhanced.

.

BALANCING INDIVIDUAL INNOVATION WITH THE TEAM

Often, innovation is associated with a bright light, an innovation leader, a lighthouse. A person.

But leading innovation is not about running every innovative project yourself, writing grand strategies, 'stakeholder involvement' and five-year plans.

It's about showing an understanding of the people you're trying to bring with you and your vision, and providing space for those people to innovate around you.

When we see innovative learning environments, it's not just those with 'leader' in their job title who are pulling the shots.

All too often we also see that, somehow, members of the learning community have become leaders in their own right.

At Milpitas public school district on the outskirts of San Francisco, 10,000 students enjoy the kind of innovative, student-led, technology-assisted, inspiring learning about which many educators can only dream. The district achieved this with a strategy that did not span years but months. In less than two years, this district has become a stellar story of transformation in state schools, with visitors flocking from overseas to see how a Silicon Valley school with more than 50% immigrant population creates such an innovative environment for learning.

What do they discover? The school district achieved this thanks to the ideas and plan of its teachers.

The story is described by the district Superintendent:

'Districts usually take years to plan and produce a binder that sits on a shelf. But binders do not change the system,' says district Superintendent Cary Matsuoka. So two years ago, Matsuoka asked his district teachers and principals one simple question: 'If you could design a school what would it look like?'

'After a three-month design process in the spring of 2012, Milpitas teachers were ready to pitch their new models to Matsuoka, his executive cabinet and the teachers' union. The result: two-thirds of elementary school classrooms are now implementing blended learning, 3,500 Chromebooks have been dispersed across the district, and data points are being collected on 7,000 students every day with iReady software. Here's how it happened.'

Matsuoka was inspired in 2012 by the process of design thinking, which provides broad parameters and a human-centred approach to rethinking the way things are done, the way things are built, and how people might use services and products.

By refocussing on people, rather than strategies, nearly two-thirds of schools in the district have been able to recalibrate learning, creating engaging, happy places with improved engagement.

But for many school leaders dipping their toes (and their Google searches) into design thinking, it is, at best, a vague notion that comes as an add-on to traditional strategy approaches and, at worst, an over-simplified process that leads to mediocre, small-scale change.

In the chapters ahead, we will harness the process of design thinking and reveal many tactics that help facilitate the kinds of discussions and staff-student-parent empowerment that a story like Matsuoka's reveals.

Beyond the post-it notes and LEGO of your average design thinking introduction, we explore how education organisations can create powerful, empowering strategies that evolve naturally within changing world around us.

HAPPY LEARNING

Take a moment to recollect your happiest memories as you learned something new.

What were you doing? What kind of activity were you undertaking?

Some of the thousands of educators to whom I've put this question sometimes talk of moments of academic success – gaining the best grade – but have to think twice when we insist on memories of actual moments of learning. Rarely do they remember learning anything the day they got the grade, and many, frankly, can't even remember what it was they had learned to get that stellar grade.

Instead, the happiest moments of the 8000+ young people, mums, dads, parents and business people I've asked this question are remarkably similar.

Often out top: Making Stuff.

Closely behind are school trips – learning that took place far away from school, or out in the school garden.

Others talk in more abstract terms about when they felt they could choose what they did next, or followed a truly personal passion. Nearly everyone remembers a passionate teacher.

This simple exercise is a great way to find out whether the people around you 'get' what great learning is about.

High Tech High founder, Larry Rosenstock, undertakes a similar task with community members and teachers:

You say to everyone: 'Would you please spend five or ten minutes, and write down your two most memorable learning experiences from your high school years'. And then you ask them: 'Will you please all discuss those memorable learning experiences and come up with the key characteristics that define what was an important significant learning experience for you all?

And then you're going to get up and share those and I'm going to be up at this chart here and I'm going to write down what they were.'

I've done this in about 28 cities. I've been tempted sometimes to write down like a card trick person what they were going to say because I know what they were going to say. What they say is that:

- ✓ *it was a project*
- ✓ *it involved community*
- ✓ *it had fear of failure*
- ✓ *it had recognition of success*
- ✓ *it had a mentor*
- ✓ *it had a public display of work*

It had all of the things that High Tech High is based on... How does this comport with the way you teach and if it doesn't comport with the way you teach what can we then do to get you teaching the way you yourself learned?

Again it wasn't imposed on you this came from within you. That's a great place to start with communities. It's a great place to start with teachers.

When we shine the light back on the status quo, the way things are done today, those opportunities that we held so dear in our own learning experiences are rare.

The moments that we count as our happiest as learners seem few and far between. Very few high school students make something every day as they learn, beyond an essay that is.

School trips are often at the end of the school year, a reward for learning well done but with modest

How To Come Up With Great Ideas and Actually Make Them Happen

expectations of learning to take place, and certainly little that is purposefully connected to curriculum or assessed for understanding later, even informally.

In the hierarchy of learning, it's not 'serious' learning that happens on a trip. And as for student choice in the direction learning might take, of the thousands of educators I've asked very few are able to say with conviction that they see a large degree of student choice in what they learn, how they learn it, where and when.

The teacher has generally decided that for them in the lesson plan on Sunday night. Schools, it seems, tend to fail to translate what we all know we love when we learn into some kind of system whereby there is a sense of entitlement and guarantee in students' learner experience.

And as for more quantifiable research being translated into classroom action, there is a raft of perceived red tape, apathy or lack of time getting in the way. After all, how many schools operate on a 'no grades, just comments' basis, or employ the 'no hands up (unless you have a question)' rule?

Both show significant evidence of positive impact on learning, but are still perceived as so innovative as to be difficult or impossible to implement swiftly. Schools, districts and entire countries often have long-term strategies, composed to stretch five or more years into the future.

The people who write them come and go, and the text in a school district strategy may be read by fewer than 100 people, and certainly not by the parents, students and many of the teachers who will put it into action.

Still, we need these documents for a variety of reasons, whether to guarantee funding, keep a Board happy, or simply to tick someone else's box.

But it's not strategy documents that make happy, challenging, choice-filled, successful learning. It's not strategy documentation that makes innovation happen.

Innovation and engaging learning happen thanks to

people feeling engaged enough to go and do more than the status quo and business-as-usual. Rather than simply rely on the one strategy document for a whole school or district into which so much effort is poured, a sprinkling of goodwill and a drop of luck, schools need to work out an additional strategy that sits alongside, or under, their five-year vision documents.

An Innovation Strategy would be written in human language, underpinned by shared tactics, tools and ideas that show the way and empower people to innovate within feasible parameters of scope, scale and ambition.

An Innovation Strategy is a pragmatic strategy that informs everyone in a school community what their role is in making the school's ambition come true, and what their first steps might be.

We need an Innovation Strategy that doesn't just reach for the stars, but shows you which smaller galaxies we might want to visit first to get there.

BUT WE'RE DOING SO WELL…

One of the most frequent rebuttals of any change or innovation in education is that any given school, district or school system is already doing rather well.

Somewhere, someone will find the statistic to justify the current means of working: good grades.

The same attitude towards success was evident a decade ago in the newspaper industry, as, on a commercial high, editors and publishers refused to believe that they'd be hurt by an internet that had already had a whole decade, at least, to do its worst damage to their industry.

How wrong could they have been? Journalist Scott Anthony describes how, back in early 2005, he and colleague Clark Gilbert ran a workshop for 100 top executives in the US newspaper industry:

The sentiment in the room was clearly triumphant. Pundits had proclaimed that the newspaper industry was a shuffling dinosaur as the commercial Internet took off in the late 1990s, yet most companies still had healthy financial statements and stable balance sheets.

We saw it differently, describing to industry leaders the need to radically change in response to disruptive content models (later that year, Huffington Post and YouTube were founded) and emerging advertising models like Google's search-based advertising.

Industry leaders were buoyant because advertising revenues continued to grow over the next couple of years. But the warning signs were in plain sight.

Readership had been dipping for four successive generations, as most youth turned to social networks and other online media for news.

Advertising spending was shifting, albeit more slowly than readers were changing their behavior. For example, a prescient report by McKinsey in 2005 showed that classified advertisement (the true driver of profitability for many newspaper companies) had decoupled from newspapers' economic growth.

Executives dismissed the argument... proclaiming McKinsey's analysis 'shallow and superficial'.

When the industry tipped, it did so with a fury... 60 years of growth was wiped out in three.

So, much like we can learn in retrospect what happened to the newspaper industry, we can take a look at what, today, remain the key motivations, biases and experiences that prevent or slow down change in the status quo of learning.

I started teaching in 1999, which is not really that long ago. Even in this short period, we've seen two economic crashes and the growth of the internet from 200m users, twice as many in the US as the rest of the world together, to nearly 4 billion, spanning the globe, with the US now a relatively minor player in the user base.

Since 2003 I've seen my world of interest expand from the classroom to the world of creative internet startups, investment in risky ideas and the transformation of once ailing global companies into global giants.

I wanted to find out why education seemed to have a slower pace of change than these other industries in which I ended up working.

French philosopher and anthropologist Pierre Bourdieu has put forward a trilogy of reasons for this lack of pace in change, and not just for schools but in many other domains too: field, habits and identity.

The field is where what we're informed by research as being good learning and teaching is thrown out in the hubbub and busy-ness of the school day: 'Forget what they tell you about teaching at Uni – this is where you'll find out how to really teach.'

To get over this, the whole field needs to experience the changes being proposed to remove pressure to descend to lowest common denominator.

The lowest common denominator in the field? Every time? Yes – because the habitus of the people in the field is formed from the strong experiences of learning at school, the thirteen years compulsory schooling that shapes our inner understanding of what a successfully run classroom or school looks like.

When we enter the classroom again, in our twenties, thirties or forties, it is this strong visual (and odoursome) memory that kicks back in, and we revert to the way we were taught. This is why it's important to always know what our happiest and least happy memories were at school, and work out ways to emulate the former and change the latter.

Finally, the identity of a teacher is formed from this collective mix of historical habitus and current-day field – individual responsibility for development within the collective responsibility for change as a whole school is the only way to adapt for the long haul.

The need for educators to think differently about innovation has been well documented, and not just in 'Western' education systems (whatever they might constitute now; in my mind, Western is interchangeable with 'too slow').

Charlie Leadbeater has uncovered several 'under the radar' examples from Africa, India and South America that have shown innovative methods dating back decades.

Some, one might say, are leapfrogging the current debates on what might be 'the right way' to innovate in schools.

In his book, *Innovation in Education*, Leadbeater suggests that the time has come, with the gift of easier collaboration through the internet, we could perhaps begin to form a system for innovation that moves beyond 'charismatic individuals' and towards, instead, 'a step-by-step guide, product or system' for innovation in learning:

... Systems need innovation to be self-motivated, coming from within rather than forced from outside, with a student-centric approach at their core...

... Are systems able to close the innovation gap by continually feeding educators and the system with fresh ideas, methods, tools, organisational models for learning?

... We need more systematic ways to promote radical forms of innovation, to create new models of learning that go beyond and challenge orthodox schooling.

... International flows of ideas are vital to feeding innovation. The more ideas there are the more connections, the more chance of finding the idea(s) that will bring success.

Through the work of investing in, advising on and building up dozens of companies in the past three years, I've begun to see that much of what the digital media world seeks in its startup founders is also what we seek in our young people.

These startups revolve primarily around one central systemic understanding: the understanding of failure and success.

It's systemic because everyone in the field has experienced failure and success intimately. Whether you are with a startup in Mumbai, London or San Francisco, that knowledge of how to harness failure to create future success is embedded in systems and ways of working that are remarkably similar, regardless of geography.

This shared experience has transformed their methods of work, and large corporations are now seeing that not thinking like Google (anything is possible), not thinking like Facebook (connecting people has value) or not thinking like Zappos (your employees are number one priority and the rest follows) will lead to their best talent drifting away, their best ideas being buried in corporate America's equivalent of high stakes testing: the demands of quarterly earnings reports and annual figures for the stock market.

But the way we go about creating successful creative digital companies seems not yet to have rubbed off on the education world. The world of schooling is still geared towards those quarterly earnings reports of grades, tests and reporting.

This book explores the attitudes of coders, programmers, designers, fashion merchandisers, Chief Executive Officers, marketers and finance officers who have seen their ideas fail, and succeed, and what habits they have found lead to success.

The startup strategies and tactics in this book work incredibly well in the world of education, and offer a nimble way for leaders, innovators and students alike to develop their new ideas in better ways and begin to better overcome the gravitational pull of field, habitus and identity. Taken together, they can help school leaders and innovators in schools, and those who lead innovation without the word 'leader' in their job title.

They help you work out if your nascent innovative ideas are really needed, how they need to change to have more chance of success, and suggest strong pragmatic steps to gain impact from your idea among those who will benefit most from its introduction.

MOVING BEYOND ISLANDS OF EXCELLENCE

'Yes, what is it like? Certainly not like she dreamed. But maybe that's okay. We want what we want. At home, she works herself into a frenzy worrying about what she isn't – and perhaps loses track of just where she is.'
Jess Walter, *Beautiful Ruins*

Ewan McIntosh

THE CHALLENGE OF 'ONE-ROOM INNOVATION'

In 2002, I was teaching French and German at a high school in the east of Scotland, on the outskirts of Edinburgh. Musselburgh Grammar School is a comprehensive state school in the local authority, or school district, of East Lothian.

The school serves a wide range of students, their motivation for learning a foreign language ranging from those who want to emigrate to a land of foreign tongues before their sixteenth birthday to those who are quite vocal in their insistence that they have no intention of ever visiting any country outside Musselburgh.

There were times when, for some of them, the city of Edinburgh, six miles away, felt like a foreign country.

In 2002, as now, engaging them in learning a language they might never speak, from countries they may never visit, was a tall order.

Traditional teaching methods of textbook as the foundation, teacher-led games and activities as the practice and worksheets as the extension were the norm. I had been taught to teach a high-paced lesson, never letting students take too much slack on their own, independent learning limited mostly to 'carousel'-type activities that were neither too in-depth nor too time-consuming.

The name of the game was pushing kids through a high-paced sausage factory of learning.But things changed.

Within six weeks of starting my job there, I was fortunate enough, as part of a vacation study visit, to visit

New Brunswick classrooms and gain an understanding of their French immersion programmes, where interaction and student-led learning were the norm.

The contrast was a sharp one, and my teaching changed overnight as a consequence. Some of the innovations I wanted to start were simple, but ambitious for the context.

I didn't want students to speak any English, just the foreign language. I wanted students to learn through projects that were meaningful to them, not just crunch their way through vocabulary themes set at some point in the nineteenth century, led by a textbook publisher's idea of 'logical' areas of language to learn.

I wanted students to use the language 'for real', through their projects but also through ongoing collaboration and exchange between their classes and students elsewhere around the French- and German-speaking world. I wanted to use weblogs to facilitate these connections, and to better share the school expeditions to the beaches of Normandy or the concentration camps of Auschwitz, and the sights and sounds of Paris, with the wider school community back home.

I wanted to create a website that would provide one port of call for all those weblogs, and all the digital material that was emerging to support language learners at home and in class.

We were front-page news on national newspapers, as our school became known for some of the most innovative blog use in the country, one of the world's first ever podcasts (and the first in Europe from a secondary school) and a raft of vibrant, busy school weblogs that spanned over twenty country links.

The school was winning national and international awards for its collaborative ventures, with ceremonies in London, Paris and more newspaper stories. It sounds like a head teacher's dream.

All of this innovation was great for students' self-esteem (and their teacher's), and engaged more students in foreign language learning, doing better than their predicted grades would have it. But it all happened very much within my own room, 'inside the Black Box' as Dylan Wiliam and Paul Black's formative assessment masterpiece is titled.

For three years, little of the language learning innovation or technology innovations crept beyond my circle of control or influence, beyond my classroom door. My classroom might as well have been a 'Black Box', or black hole, into which all the innovative ideas I came up with and practised disappeared. People were aware of what was going on, but few were empowered to take up those ideas themselves. There was a problem. I was fast approaching burnout, taking on more and more of the infrastructure, equipment requests and bid-writing.

The school – and I – lacked an innovation strategy that could cope with these new ideas within the framework of existing strategy and initiatives. Anything new was considered 'just one more thing' to add to an overcrowded agenda, and in spite of the best efforts of colleagues, it was always going to be hard to revel in going deep into these innovations.

The term 'new innovations', that is, innovative ideas that come along outside the frame of the annual planning process, would be a pleonasm in any other context: of course innovations are new! But in schools, and in my school at that time, any 'new innovations' had little chance of growing, spreading and lasting.

Leadership and teaching staff could invest their time, energy, money or mental bandwidth in only the 'old innovations' that had been planned for within the annual and five-year plans.

The result? A school filled with people like me, doing innovative new things within their black box, behind closed doors, unable to spread and grow their ideas beyond that incubator. A sea filled with islands of excellence, and no means to travel between them, let alone connect them into a continent.

JOINED UP THINKING

ISLANDS OF EXCELLENCE: HOW DO YOU BEGIN TO JOIN THEM UP?

A few years later, I ended up working across the whole school district of East Lothian, with the goal of increasing the sharing of teachers' resources, lesson ideas and thinking about teaching and learning.

Albeit that the district is small, with 45 geographically spread out schools, I was aware of the challenges of innovating within just one school. How was our team of four ICT specialists to gain the trust, excitement, time, energy, effort and attention for 'new innovations' from 45 schools, each with their own 'old innovations', five year plans and competing policies?

Having learned firsthand the drawbacks of not having an innovation strategy to help people harness new ideas, particularly those involving technology, my team this time around met with more success.

We worked out the barriers to getting adoption of our ideas: namely time and the fear of spending that time on something that might not bring value to the teacher personally.

We worked out what made other people want to adopt any new technology or idea: their friends are using it, they see others' classes being engaged by it.

We wrote down those fears and needs as 'innovation ingredients', and designed a modest programme of events and online action to meet those desires.

How To Come Up With Great Ideas and Actually Make Them Happen

What was the challenge?

Over the course of our first year we broke down the barriers of fear of losing time and expectation of immediate success, one school at a time, by gaining the support of leaders first and foremost.

We found their two key 'pains' were nearly uniformly shared at that time:

1. Leaders shared a lack of expertise in knowing what could and could not be done through online publishing, and in their ignorance had more often than not opted towards complacency (deciding not to actively encourage publishing and online sharing of learning and teaching) or in some cases conservatism (banning it).

2. Leaders had seen nearly a decade of mostly failed technology initiatives with large price tags. They wanted to protect their time-poor staff from more of the same.

To redraw the lines of strategy school by school would have taken forever, and a change in policy would be unlikely to create practical, fast change on a classroom level. School strategy was set, in any case.

We needed to create an Innovation Strategy that could weave in between 45 existing school strategies, preferably unnoticed, and which led to pragmatic action on the ground. Its purpose would be to help each group of teachers in each school to cope with new ways of learning and teaching with (and without) technologies and the opportunities this brought.

What did we do?

This innovation journey did not feel like a strategy at the time – little was written down and there was next to no documentation to tell people what to do: you know, the ones with sub-sections and more bullets than the Bourne Identity.

Our Innovation Strategy, if we could have called it that, was based on meeting the key needs we had identified.

We decided to appeal to the existing time within the Continuing Professional Development (CPD) calendar by starting a 'TeachMeet Roadshow'. These technology-focussed sessions were a 'canned' service that schools could request from the central ICT team.

They were themed on a specific technology or creative task that schools had expressed a strong desire to use in school, but which lack of time, budget or mental bandwidth had thwarted from happening: podcasting, movie-making, sharing through blogs, digital photography, clay animation.

Each Roadshow happened in two hours, at the end of the school day.

The usual approach for a centralised ICT team of four people is to spread out, cover several schools simultaneously with a traditional 'show and tell' type format.

We flipped that notion, and arrived for each Roadshow en masse, four people for each small staff team of around 30-50 people.

This meant that one-on-one time was possible with small in-school teams of three teachers working together. The quality of dialogue was higher than the traditional lecture, show and tell format as a result.

There was little 'teaching': each session began with a 20-minute unpicking of an example animation or podcast, for example, that illustrated 'what a good one looks like'.

We reverse-engineered what had gone into it, and then left up to one hour for the teachers to explore, to play, something that had been expressed in our research as a rare commodity in schools. Finally, we had 30 minutes of exposition, celebrating the first efforts in animation, publishing or podcasting that had just taken place.

The sessions were incredibly simple in design, but each element had been tied to our unwritten strategy:

practitioner-led, fitting within the constraints of existing time, a sense of entitlement to an 'event' for the whole school to undertake together.

The logic was that every teacher learning about the same concept would allow more peer-to-peer help later, once we had left.

We insisted on the whole school participating, and made clear that we would pack up and go if any one educator felt that they had something more urgent to do.

In the end, staff really enjoyed that sense of collegiality, of everyone learning together and from each other.

Above all, we quashed the second leadership challenge we had heard about in our research: for the first time in a long time for many, their teaching staff were succeeding together with a 'new innovation', and it had cost nothing to do.

There was no Big Strategy document, but there was a 'good idea' at its core, we thought, and we had discussed at length the things we knew mattered if we wanted to see our innovations adopted en masse.

All that was left now for the school to do, was to place a request for a loan of equipment for that month to start trying, prototyping what they had learned in the TeachMeet Roadshow with real live children in their classrooms.

In the course of one year we demolished any target that might have been set for getting teachers sharing their learning.

From a standing start of 20 out of 1500 staff sharing what they did through weblogs, within six months we had 800 – over half – sharing movies, photographs, audio and text about how children learn in their classrooms.

From a teacher-focussed proposition – that is, 'get teachers sharing' – we began to see exemplar practice in having students share what they were learning in class. Visitor statistics on the school weblogs were fascinating to explore.

As the number of weblogs grew, with more teachers and students sharing their learning, so, too, did the number of people looking at them. There were peaks of traffic at around 2pm and 10pm. This audience was not students (in bed) or teachers (at work), but parents – 2pm, before picking their children up from school, parents were able to see what they had been learning that day.

Conversations at the school gate went from 'What did you do at school today?' to 'Tell me all about this pirates project!'. And we can only guess that the 10pm crowd were also parents, and perhaps teacher peers, peering in once their own children were tucked up. We affectionately called this group the 'shiraz brigade', as they relaxed for the first time in the day and took to seeing what their children had been experiencing.

Several head teachers commented on how conversations with parents had become more frequent, more informed, and more useful all round.

Still today, the blog servers of East Lothian serve between 3.5m and 4.5m pages every month, helping local communities gel around their school, helping improve conversations about learning between professionals and between parents.

FROM MYSTERY TO ALGORITHMIC INNOVATION

Arguably, much of our work in East Lothian was a mix of luck, created by listening hard and often to what people in the community were saying.

My colleague at the time, David Gilmour, was an expert listener, and continues to this day to tweak not only the online offerings for teachers across the district, but also the professional development offerings for them.

But there are more structured mechanisms to avoid luck alone, and the street pounding that David and the rest of the team undertook.

After three years in Government working on projects like those in East Lothian, I went on to experience innovation with Channel 4 Television Corporation and various regional investment agencies across the country, investing millions in technology ideas that would bring public services to the masses. The setting was totally different – and not directly related to education at all – but the challenges were remarkably similar.

Part of the downside of working with and investing in startups is that you have to hear a never-ending stream of good ideas, and not all of them are the next Facebook – far from it, in fact.

Over the past five years, in my capacity as an investor or advisor for media companies, I've read through over 3000 ideas from innovators, entrepreneurs, business people and public servants. All of them think their idea is innovative.

Only 30 have seen their idea receive investment. Only a dozen or so of these have made any money worth talking about. One is consistently in Apple's Top 30 all-time best-selling games list.

This might sound like a low success rate, and it is, but the advantage of expending real effort on so few ideas is that those which succeed do so in grand style.

The advantage for the 2970 or so others is that they receive regular critique on why certain ideas might work better than others.

In the world of education, it sometimes feels like the opposite is true. Most schools and their teachers, leaders and school boards are paralysed by a terrible, perennial case of initiativitis.

Instead of dealing with the two or three big ideas that will make their fortune, schools seem to be expending cash, hours and energy on the 2970 other ideas that feel cute at first blush, or important for the here and now, but whose long-term value, their long-term 'business model', is debatable.

Coming up with great ideas, buying stuff and trying things out is not an Innovation Strategy. When you apply this to the 2970 'dead' ideas it is also incredibly costly and demoralising.

Trial and error discussions, like those we undertook in East Lothian district, are not an Innovation Strategy either. Neither approach is systemic, and both rely on the wits, experience and luck of those invested in making the idea come about.

To move ideas beyond their islands of excellence, out of the black box of the classroom, we need something that is more reliable.

TAKING IDEAS BEYOND THE BLACK BOX

At Canada's Rotman School of Management, Professor Roger Martin has spent time trying to work out systems for making creative and critical thinking in innovation projects more predictable, more 'systematised'.

Martin describes the 'knowledge funnel' of every organisation. At the beginning of any new idea or innovation, much of the organisation sees that innovation as 'mystery' – it's unknown, perceived as unimportant perhaps, or even dangerous to the organisation. As more is learned about an idea by those in the organisation, that knowledge forces a better understanding, one of gut feel, instinctual understanding of the new idea – 'heuristics'.

It is only once knowledge about the idea has become a strong enough foundation, an understanding about which the organisation doesn't have to think too hard, that we can talk about 'algorithmic' understanding of the innovation, and it's often at this point that we see innovations adopted on a much larger scale.

This pushing of knowledge through the funnel demands that some of the initial complexity and nuance of an innovation might be lost:

Algorithms demand stripping away extraneous ideas and the potential of possibility. It's hard to reverse back up the knowledge funnel once ideas have been stripped away. They're often lost forever.

We see this clearly with technology innovation. In the early days of blogging, there was a bunch of subtleties and complexity in creating, maintaining and growing a loyal readership of the blog – innovators were those who, frankly, could write well, often and about interesting things, but who could also code and manage the searchability of their text.

I remember a twelve-year-old kid in my class, Hassan, editing my hand-coded XML in order to get podcasts appearing in iTunes.

One-click publishing in 2004 was really three clicks and some code. Today, many of those skills are just not required as the technological interface for publishing online is seamless, and more people are used to the processes involved.

Today's 'new innovations' build on the 'old innovations' that many of us struggled through in the first part of the century. But today's 'new innovations' can also mean the loss of some of that subtlety from the early days.

More people 'blog' on Twitter, 140 characters at a time, than spend a morning crafting a long-form blog post.

The 'half life' of a text online has been reduced from maybe a week of commenting, interaction and replies on a 2004 blog, to minutes of retweeting, replies and reading on Twitter.

Writing a good tweet is not the same kind of writing as forming a 600- or 6000-word blog post.

But what Twitter, Facebook and other social networks have allowed is a growth in the numbers of people sharing something, anything, online, because doing so has become possible without thinking. It has gone from something that was mysterious (a few people did it), to heuristic (a lot of interesting great writers do it) to algorithmic (nearly everyone seems to be doing it, but we pay the price in some of what we see from them being less routinely of interest or of higher quality).

DO WE LOSE GREAT IDEAS WHEN WE GROW THEM?

The danger with this kind of scale is that some of the 'magic' of an initial idea may, and probably will, be lost.

The innovator in their classroom is often unconsciously reluctant, in fact, to share their ideas widely for fear of having them watered down, or lost in the inevitable conformity of 'the system'.

And it is the outlandish ideas, the circles that don't quite fit the existing square, that can provide the big breakthrough innovations we want to harness.

For example, take Dr Scherer at the Hospital for Sick Children in Toronto, a researcher into autism who is trying to find a cure for millions of children and adults.

To do this, he plots autism data from research on a chart. Most scientists would logically concentrate on the majority of cases, trying to find trends and similarities that might lead to a cure for those masses. They would concentrate on the 2970 other ideas.

Scherer is different. He goes for the 'outlandish cases, the ones ignored by research as extraneous or fluke results', as these are the cases where often the cure could be found.

Charles Leadbeater calls this The Predilection Gap – the meeting between analytical and intuitive thinking, specificity and flexibility.

It is in this often large chasm where some of the best innovations are born, and it is in this gap that school leaders, innovators and creatives love to operate.

But to thrive in the gap, one needs an Innovation Strategy, a few stepping stones, a safety net and a jetpack to move from the status quo on one side to the big hairy ambitious goals that lie beyond the gap, on the horizon.

THE THREE HORIZONS

Throughout the book, as a way of thinking about the stages of innovation, we will use the metaphor of 'The Three Horizons'. The Three Horizons is a metaphor on which an Innovation Strategy can be successfully built, helping us move from the horizon of the status quo to a new horizon, in the distance. McKinsey consultants and others have for thirty years talked about the Three Horizons of Innovation:

Horizon One is the here-and-now, the initiatives that take up our time today. Horizon Three is that far-off-feeling place of the innovations that the organisation needs to undertake to guarantee its future. **Horizon Two** is the transition period where, in theory at least, Horizon One type activities are phased out as **Horizon Three** type activities take their place.

Rarely is that second horizon smooth, and most education innovations, in reality, fail to push the first horizon out of the field of vision of leaders, colleagues, parents or even students alike.

Horizon One, that place of current politics and policies, getting through each day, each term, each school year and being content with having simply managed to keep on top of that, this first horizon might be described as the innovator's lead weight.

Nor are the one-time innovative activities of Horizon One necessarily worth keeping. In fact, in education, we have a perennial habit of snapping what we do in Horizon

How To Come Up With Great Ideas and Actually Make Them Happen

One and replacing it with equally unambitious or poorly thought through innovations that do not constitute the excitement and future-affirming feel of Horizon Three innovations. Or, more often, we try to shoehorn Horizon Three grand ideas into the confines of Horizon One's current thinking.

One of the key things we tend to associate with innovation is coming up with ideas. We will see in the course of our innovation journey that this is a relatively short and swift part of a process that, first and foremost, is about identifying very specifically the people whom we can work to benefit the most.

The ideas for meeting their needs can only come after we've defined those needs and drawn out a clear idea of who needs them the most. Because innovation in education in the past has often been so rarely about the people involved, it is no surprise that we point to so few educational innovations that have stood the test of time for a fraction as long as those we see in the technological, engineering, design or creative worlds: the Burberry trenchcoat (1857, and more popular today than ever); the Dyson vacuum cleaner (the result of 5126 failed prototypes before it); the Eiffel Tower (designed to stay one year, and still there 120 years on).

In schools, ideas are often assumed innovative when they are not, and plenty of genuinely innovative ideas are ignored. The inclusion or absence of technology has increasingly become the mistaken indicator of innovation, the practice of students and teachers – the evidence of actual learning – less so.

Whether or not an idea contains technology, its definition as innovative or not depends on a journey that starts well before the press releases, blog posts and gushing praise from the Edutopia website. The most innovative ideas begin their lives in the same way, through the same actions of the entrepreneurial thinkers behind them:

- Innovative people relentlessly search for big problems that people care about and no one has yet solved particularly well. They ignore problems that don't matter so much to the people they affect.
- Innovative ideas come both in the shower and around the boardroom table. A mixture of approaches is seen as the only way to guarantee a consistently satisfactory idea quota.
- Innovative leaders know how to frame creative argument, in order to create better ideas, involve more people and maintain ownership of the idea by the person or people who came up with it.
- Innovators know how to 'sell' their ideas, but are never too precious about the ideas themselves. Indeed, they crave feedback and work fast to change their ideas based on how they actually go down 'in the real world'.
- Innovators bring together diverse teams to deliver their idea, and often to manage it. But as entrepreneurial thinkers, they know their role in leading it.

NEXT STEPS... GETTING SET UP

- ✓ What can you do to reduce the perception that 'leaders' are the only people who do the leading in your organisation? Are your job titles a help or a hindrance? Do you have a design team for each new task on the plan which is made up and owned by junior members of staff, or even students?

- ✓ Who is currently innovating solely within their four walls? Create a list, and get them together to start acting as an innovation team to develop ideas together.

- ✓ In Milpitas district the community was asked simply: 'If you could design a school what would it look like?' How many goals do your students and teachers have? How many questions are they expected to answer at any one time? Can you find a key question that the school is concentrated upon for any given period of time?

- ✓ Undertake a 'happiest learning moments' discussion with your team.

- ✓ What are the habitat, identity and field that you and your team currently occupy? What are some of the hurdles you will have to jump over at some point?

THE FIRST HORIZON: ASSUME NOTHING

'Humans see what they want to see'
Rick Riordan, *The Lightning Thief*

How To Come Up With Great Ideas and
Actually Make Them Happen

SETTING UP YOUR COLLABORATIVE TEAM

Funnily enough, the first step on your innovation journey is not deciding what you're going to innovate on. It's to bring together a team who represent the institution and the people it serves.

The team's day jobs should play second fiddle to the fact that they are (a) representative of a group of people, regardless of their pay grade and (b) keen to be part of a process of innovation, and not just about getting their job done.

This is important, because nearly always innovation projects start a large degree of uncertainty, or 'mystery', before research and team learning begins to make sense of the data coming in, and people learn new skills on the way. This process takes mystery to 'heuristics', or rules of thumb that are commonly understood but hard to articulate.

The team begins to reach common understandings about the way things work, and why, but find it hard to explain this to new members of the team or outsiders. It is only when a team have gone through this ambiguous phase that clarity can emerge and an 'algorithmic' understanding of the process appears, that is, the ways of working and the learnings generated through the project become second nature to those participating in it.

The opposite to this occurring happens all the time in innovation projects in schools: people start out with enthusiasm and, when the project gets difficult or hits an apparent brick wall, they leave, one by one, until only the die-hard enthusiasts are left.

Therefore, to get people from the excitement of mystery through the hard work of turning that into rules of thumb, or heuristics, before eventually bringing innovation to the masses as it becomes more algorithmic, we need willing team members, who understand the journey ahead. Roger Martin, a Rotman University Professor who specialises in design thinking in the corporate sphere, puts the challenge in team formation this way:

> *In most organisations people have defined job titles, meaning that they take responsibility for themselves and their work (my responsibilities) instead of for the task in hand. The activity of moving knowledge through the funnel runs against most people's logic if it means that their job responsibility becomes defunct. And the logical activity for making knowledge move through the funnel is the project, where everyone takes a project-specific role, roles changing with each project, playing to the (ongoing learning) strengths of each person on the team.*

According to Martin, the very idea that everyone might be working on an area that falls into one department's official remit is also a reason that people don't volunteer their efforts for truly innovative ideas: it's not in their department.

To avoid this, the possibilities of touching on various remits in an organisation have to be recognised and gulped up by the whole organisation, a result for which leadership must pave the way well in advance so as to manage expectations and the reality of the innovation process. Innovation does not respect departmental boundaries.

TEN FACES OF INNOVATION

Sometimes, it's just not possible to bring together a team for an innovation project where every member of the team represents each constituent who may benefit from the innovation.

In other cases, it might be possible but the number participating in the innovation team becomes unwieldy: you can't have a quality discussion with 20 people around a table. In this case, your innovation team may want to actively seek out different mindsets at different moments in the design cycle.

Many education and corporate spaces already make use of Edward de Bono's 'Six Hats', where team members 'wear a hat' (metaphorically) to play the role of looking at just the facts (the White Hat), the positives (Yellow Hat), playing the role of judge (Black Hat), exploring hunches and intuition (Red Hat) or creative possibilities (Green Hat), or managing the meeting (Blue Hat).

Tom Kelley of design firm IDEO proposes a more nuanced set of hats, or personas, in his work The Ten Faces of Innovation. He has noticed that many people in his design teams naturally possess one or some of these personas, and recognising where they tend to operate helps them understand where their natural skill sets might be put to best use.

But such a list of personas also helps them and their team leader to identify what personas they may have to be more active in harnessing, to see a problem or idea from the different perspective. The Personas are split into three broad categories.

The Learning Personas are particularly useful in the First Horizon, as they are about setting the scene, digesting facts, seeing things from different perspectives:

The Anthropologist
is the mindset of getting out into the field to see how people actually do what they do, rather than just assuming we know what they do. They gather data, perspectives and facts to bring back to the base for digestion later on. Key to their attitude is a strong sense of empathy, seeing things

from the perspectives of others, and reframing problems along different lines.

The Experimenter
constantly tests and retests how certain ideas might play out, bringing people in to join this journey of enlightened trial and error.

The Cross-Pollinator
brings seemingly unrelated ideas or information together to create new insights. They are naturally curious and maven-like, not hesitating to bring ideas from one sector into another to see how they might connect.

The Organizing Personas lend themselves to the process of synthesis, towards the end of the First Horizon, as we try to work out what the information gathered by our anthropological and cross-pollinating personas might mean. But they are also those roles concerned with how to actually make ideas happen: how the existing processes must play a role in making our big ideas of the Third Horizon come about:

The Hurdler
is the problem-solver who enjoys tackling those problems no one has tackled before. Like the sports people who practice this discipline, they barely seem to notice the obstacle that they must negotiate. They take constraints and help the team jump over them so that the idea can grow.

The Collaborator
values the team over the individual effort, bringing people out of existing silos to contribute to the team.

The Director
keeps the big picture in mind, and helps shape the idea so

that it will work in the long term from the starting block of the organisation's existing state.

The Building Personas are amongst the most visible in the entire innovation process, and transform innovation teams from being merely talking shops to putting ideas into action.

The Experience Architect
thinks about how real people will actually use or experience the ideas being generated by the innovation team – they have the user at heart, above all else. Having this perspective, this empathy, means that they turn potentially mediocre ideas into unique exciting experiences.

The Set Designer
helps create the physical and digital environment that will allow the innovation team to undertake their work effectively, and which will allow their ideas to flourish within the organisation.

The Storyteller
doesn't just deal in facts – they can turn those into stories that sway people's opinion, and get the idea across in such a way that captures the potential users' imaginations. They keep the idea feeling authentic, no matter how audacious it might actually be.

Finally, the Caregiver
is involved in making sure that any idea the innovation team might create actually works when it hits the road: they guide the user of the idea through the process to make sure that they have a positive experience. In the process, they may well turn Anthropologist, to feed what they discover back into the design cycle.

How To Come Up With Great Ideas and Actually Make Them Happen

Throughout the activities and process we will explore through the Three Horizons, we will make reference back to these personas. This will help your team undertake the activities with the best mindset for the task at hand.

INNOVATION UNDER YOUR NOSE

Working as a Commissioner at the television corporation for investors in the North of the United Kingdom, I'd meet with hundreds of entrepreneurs, newly formed startups and media production companies of repute, all of whom thought that they had spotted the future and had found the perfect idea to satisfy the needs of the Great British Public (and beyond). Nearly every time they had not.

There was the Google map layer that could show you hidden local walks, something that any passionate hobbiest could do for free; the platform for connecting schools across Europe, which ignored the existence of the booming eTwinning programme, funded with face-to-face events, professional development and support for tens of thousands of teachers from across the European Union.

More successful projects included a platform for artists in specific cities, starting in vibrant European cities like Glasgow and Berlin that were already rejecting the US focus of existing networks such as Behance and where artists expressed a need to connect and share work but a challenge in doing so.

ThisIsCentralStation.com continues to meet that need, and supports itself. A colleague spotted the promise in a telephone-based app that allowed you to upload, in one click, up to five minutes of audio: audioboo.fm was born. My job was to find those who maybe had, work out how much cash it would take to get the barest minimum prototype of their idea out and tested, and work out in advance what we do with it if it did show initial signs of promise.

For every 1000 ideas we received, 990 were easy to reject for, depressingly, the same reasons every time: it existed already, or there was no compelling enough need for their idea beyond their own perceived need (or, I'm sure, the perceived needs of their mum).

These companies were not daft, for the most part. They were using the experience as a sounding board to help steer them towards the next iteration of their big idea. But, for the most part, these talented folk had expended such significant effort spotting the future that they had missed the more compelling current needs of people right here, right now.

The near future needs were what the good ideas were concerned with meeting: those needs for which the Great British Public would be more than happy to hand over their hard-earned Great British Pounds to have met.

To put it bluntly, the best companies saw innovation under their noses and built their ideas fast, but the majority of inventors and creators looked to horizons so distant they had no feasible way of getting there before the lights went out on their idea.

Looking too far ahead is one danger when trying to find 'innovation'; the other is not looking at all in the present. It still amazes me how many hours, human energy and relationships are wasted in the quest to realise an idea that someone else has already invented.

Yes: a large majority of British creative talent simply failed to Google what else was out there already. More still would cite the existing competition to their idea somewhere in the pitch, pointing out the inevitable 'but ours is different/better/bigger/shinier'.

But essentially, through the lens of loving their innovation baby, they failed to understand how the competition and near-competition's very existence killed their idea before it got started.

We tend to look too far ahead when innovating for

innovating's sake is on the agenda. This mindset is triggered from many familiar innovation 'moments': writing a grant for a fund that has just become available; creating a fresh three-year strategy because the old one is about to run out; preparing a conference blurb for the distant future to present on an activity from your classroom that you've maybe not yet undertaken. These tasks are often a struggle for people, they get writer's block, as they are innovating on intellectual fumes and presumptions.

To avoid this, we need to develop a sense of what innovations are under our noses, everyday needs waiting to be met when the right moment comes along.

When the opportunity to apply for the grant arises, you have a set of genuine needs you've been waiting some time to solve.

FINDING TIME AND SCOPE TO INNOVATE

Schools are often guilty of the same dereliction of 'innovation duty', that is, they do not manage to cope with the daily minor firefights of the moment and at the same time prepare the ground for the near future.

They are so busy working 'in the business' that leadership teams struggle to work 'on the business' of where their school is headed. Instead, leadership love the vaguely Stalinistic 'Five-Year Plan'.

It feels substantial, it merits a mammoth effort, sometimes spanning not just a few terms but a few years. The advantage of forming strategy in this way is that, much like we do for children's time in a school timetable, leadership teams, teachers and others can predict when they need to make the time to deal with coming up with the new strategy, pushing 'less important' things to the side in order to achieve it.

The reality, of course, is that people are as busy as they normally are during these set, regular, predictable periods of strategy development – we end up feeling stressed by the burden of coming up with the next step, getting it right and maintaining the day-to-day to a reasonable standard all at once.

The most common complaint when it comes to taking time out to work on what a school might do in the future: 'I don't have the time.'

One school where I attempted to help on making learning more engaging had its eye on the wrong problem, in a situation many leaders, inwardly, will recognise.

The school's senior leadership had, for several years, had their headspace in the building of a totally new school complex.

This was an 'innovative' building only insofar as it was a new one – the classrooms were still classrooms, but smaller; the lack of storage was cast off as a 'design feature' (everything's going to be digitised, isn't it?); there had been and would be few playing fields or play areas for students in the three years either side of the building launch, as the new building was constructed on the former fields and the old one would have to be demolished, cleared and the grounds landscaped before over 1000 students had enough space to kick a ball away from the copious glass and steel.

The fact is, new school building projects are hefty, complex projects that few Head Teachers have been trained to manage particularly well, and even fewer deal with on a day-to-day basis.

The clue is in their job title: they are Head Teachers, not Head Project Managers, not Head Architects or Foremen or Forewomen. In this school, as I'd seen before in others, the entire senior leadership team was being sucked into a sexy role complete with hard hats and fluorescent jackets, a role for which they were poorly prepared, which sucked an insane amount of their time, energy and relationship 'bandwidth' with their staff and students.

The result of this quest for innovation in the wrong

place was revealed in an email to me from one of the leadership team, the day before I was due to meet with the rest of the leadership team and staff to talk through some ideas for developing innovation in their existing classrooms that would transfer to innovative pedagogy in their new classrooms:

> *I'm sorry, but I've had to cancel the meeting with the Senior Leadership Team... To be honest, I don't think we'll get very far [with them]... I don't think Teaching and Learning is a high priority for them.*

I believe the school leader writing this email to me was absolutely correct, and it revealed the fatal flaw in leadership placing their priorities too far ahead, not seeing how teaching and learning, the sharp end of their entire vision, can be a source for the most exciting innovation in a school, more than any shiny new building, technology roll-out or grandiose infrastructure project with a grandiose price tag.

It's not just time that is the enemy of strategy formation, but relevance too. I find it hard to imagine that over two years of writing, the strategy is as relevant today as the first day the leadership team started writing it. In fact, I've had one of my most uncomfortable days as a consultant when the school leader of a top flight independent school demanded I share 'what the next big thing in technology 20 or 50 years might be'.

It's not just that I don't know (and, neither, does any sane person; they used to throw people like that into the river to see if they floated or not). This is simply looking for innovation in the wrong place.

The great innovations for tomorrow are normally found in solving the mundane problems of today that no one else has cracked. The great innovations for tomorrow are often built on snapshots of the way things are today, not the averaged out impression of the past few months or years. And some of the best, most important innovations happen before the big bucks are spent.

INNOVATION BY PRICE TAG

Another frequent pattern is one where innovation is associated with that price tag. When I see the launch press releases of any Government initiative that focus on the sum of investment within the first paragraph, I can smell failure not too far away.

Over the past decade, various Westminster Governments in the United Kingdom have had to handle the fallout from a much lauded £12 billion National Health Service IT system, designed to save costs but, instead, costing nearly £10 billion so far with no outputs at all – the programme was scrapped in 2012.

In Scotland, home to many education innovations over the centuries, the world watched, copied and experienced the same challenges in launching centralised learning environments for whole states and countries. In Scotland, the system, today called 'Glow', was designed in the early 2000s as the Scottish Schools Digital Network and implemented around 2005-7, a time during which it was arguably known for costing a lot of money.

At the time of its conception, the idea of a unifying learning platform where students and teachers could collaborate with other schools easily, access cheap or free centrally purchased content and have a 'safe' browsing experience was revolutionary, and for most people made perfect sense.

By the time implementation came around, the online world had already changed drastically: social networks such as MySpace and Bebo dominated the scene for children of high school age. The average British family were visiting only six destination websites a day, and pushing any of the big hitters off the favourites bar was a near impossible task for sites: even a nascent Facebook struggled to get inroads to British Bebo Boomers households.

Above all, these technologies didn't cost millions to use – they were free.

Between the ideation of the new service and its implementation – between creating the vision of the Third Horizon and working out how to get there in the Second Horizon – the landscape of the First Horizon had changed beyond recognition.

The weighty strategy and decision-making processes of Government, coupled with the high price tag already invested and committed to that original plan, had no agile means of pivoting onto a new implementation journey.

And so, as well-meaning and smart people ploughed on with the plan that had originally been put in place years before, feeling empowered to make only minor alterations in their course, the foundations of the concept's sense in the marketplace were all but crumbling beneath their feet.

As they launched into the lives of 750,000 students and 53,000 educators, the launchpad had all but crumbled into the ocean.

Indeed, Glow faltered in terms of uptake: it wasn't as easy to use as the social networks in 'the real world', networks which ploughed many more millions into making their use easy, 'sticky' and connective. There have been frequent anecdotes of students trying to use Glow who could barely remember their passwords to gain entry in the first place: the usage data backs up the premise that relatively few of the potential students who could use Glow do.

In the past two years, the Scottish administration has overhauled the management of the project and set about rescoping its trajectory, mid-flight.

The journey is far from complete, but at least there's some more fuel in the ship and some more smart people at the helm. Glow and similar projects around the world today have had to deal with many more challenges to succeed than at the time when their basic concepts were being designed, barely a decade ago.

Most of these challenges cannot be met centrally, by a Government team, but require many, many people with competing agendas and bias to come together in agreement.

A key challenge is: where do students use this technology? In schools, bandwidth limitations mean that accessing the more engaging media content they provide is slow and frustrating, so many students may opt to use the service at home.

Yet, there remains a digital divide in terms of access at home in our poorest communities: policy and action on school districts' part has been lamentably slow in addressing how we get the last 12% of our nation online.

Other students still can find 'good enough' learning content on their own mobile phones, without any of the troublesome log in challenges of a school-owned system or the restrictions on the use of YouTube that still remain in many institutions.

The use of mobile phones in this way is hugely liberating for learning and knowledge discovery, but undermines the very notion of a 'national content repository': there's a free, broad international content repository just a click (and no password) away.

So, schools invest hundreds of thousands, Governments spend millions, on large-scale technology roll-out, but for years put off developing their mobile phone use policy into something that allows students to be empowered with a one-to-one personal device at zero or little cost.

It is something that is both far more mundane and, at the same time, potentially dynamite for leadership. Getting a sturdy mobile phone policy established early on means that discussions around technology infrastructure are totally different. Instead of talking hardware and content, we might start talking about equity, safe use and, above all, higher bandwidth.

Schools who have concentrated on mobile thinking first, cables, pipes and devices second, have seen far more innovative learning and teaching as a result.

Take the work of Abdul Chohan and colleagues at Essa Academy in Bolton, England. Chohan is a Chemistry Teacher turned Technology Director, helping form a new vision of learning in this school, founded in 2009 in a tough socio-economic area of the country.

The predecessor school which the Academy replaced, and in which Chohan had taught, had been close to being shut down before being injected with cash and innovation.

'I'm part of a journey with Essa Academy,' he says. 'The predecessor school hadn't had a real investment made into the fabric of the building, and there hadn't been much investment into the learning, the intellectual capital of the environment, as well. It was pretty much failing at all the usual things that schools get measured with and was about to get shut down.'

Chohan and colleagues might have gone down the route of so many others in similar conditions: on the one hand banning mobile phones in order to prevent bullying and, above all, peer pressure, while on the other hand flooding the school with many (cheaper) computers to offer 'access for all', a last ditch attempt to 'engage students through technology'.

But Chohan and colleagues' vision for learning is one based on thinking and personalisation, not just technology. It was based on learning taking place in school but in a distributed way – it's not about the teacher standing at the front of the class delivering the same thing to all.

Very quickly [as we worked out the vision for the new Academy] we decided that there was only going to be one thing that was going to happen: that every student who comes here will succeed. This wasn't just in a tokenistic sense, we mean at all levels: in terms of their ability, the investment we put in and what students get when they leave the academy in terms of academics and in terms of preparing for their uncertain futures

How To Come Up With Great Ideas and Actually Make Them Happen

in jobs that don't yet exist.

We wanted to move away from the idea that we're a "school" to "this is where learning happens". We didn't want to be an institution where students come and things are done to them. It meant moving away from the usual approaches where students are categorised by their date of manufacture.

I came across the iPod Touch, which did what I wanted it to do: it wasn't a phone, and it would work wirelessly. We started out with a project where we'd give each student an iPod Touch. There was uproar initially. But one of the first things I started to notice early on were the creative things that students were doing, and which I was learning from. Staff were beginning to pick up ideas from students, seeing this creativity happening between students.

For example, there was one girl, Anna, from Poland. A fantastic student, really good at sciences, though her English wasn't great yet. The traditional way of working with these students had been to remove kids like Anna from science to teach them English, then put them back in the science class and expect them to catch up and do well.

She asked not to come out of science. She'd come in with her iPod Touch, look up the reference materials on Wikipedia – in Polish – on her iPod Touch. She would understand the principle of, say, the electric motor, but she's also learned some of the English language from the teacher. When she leaves the room, she has improved her English but she's also done fantastically well, in the end, at understanding scientific concepts.

Students come to us, the teachers, and say: "Look what I can do!" It's the students who are teaching us how to harness these small devices using creative commons images to explain what they want to do, eat or that they want to go to the toilet.

More boys downloaded examination revision podcasts to their device than girls – 9000 downloads in total over the examination period. They were able to learn for and by themselves, without having to see the teacher as the fount of all knowledge.

> *There were huge savings in time, effort and money, too. Caretakers and other admin staff would do a job in one place, run to the computer on the other side of the campus to pick up another job, only to find out that they had to go all the way back to where they had been for the task – with the iPod Touch, the efficiency of being able to look up the next job on the spot was clear. As for student planners – which students hate to use, and which cost £6250 – we just use the calendars on the device. Printing and printers had cost £40,000 per year. We won't need anywhere near as much. The costs of the innovation are low: 18 pence (30 cents) per day per student. It's do-able.*

This is truly innovative, even a few years after its initial implementation, since it continues to provide an environment on which innovative learners, innovative teachers and innovative leadership can build.

The results are not just financial – in the first year of implementation of this innovation, academic results improved to the point where Grades awarded A*-C stood at 99% of students; English and Maths results at A*-C stood at 52% where traditionally the school had never breached a 30% pass rate. The local press didn't believe the results.

Certainly, the building the technology is housed within is a stunning one, but the innovation is not the building. The building is not what people travel around the world to see. The learning that goes on inside is, and much of this student-focussed approach to learning and teaching stemmed from Chohan and colleagues looking in the right place for the problem that needed solving – that is, when teachers lead too much of the learning, these students get disengaged, therefore we must provide means for them to learn more independently, and to take more of a lead in teaching each other.

How To Come Up With Great Ideas and Actually Make Them Happen

If you just give an iPod Touch to every student in any old way it doesn't happen. We focused on pedagogy and personalisation of learning for the student. Students were able to take exams when they were ready, not when they are dictated. It meant that we had students taking exams early – talented Grade 8s sitting their exams with Grade 11s – and vice versa.

So, for leaders and innovators who receive big budgets for their grand ideas, the lesson might be 'buyer beware'. It's essential to gain an understanding of the real underlying issues that prevent people achieving what they might first, as more often than not 'buying stuff' will not meet those fundamental needs: thinking them through will.

WHEN DO YOU DECIDE TO START INNOVATING?

Most grand innovations that we hear about in the education world are the result of a planned innovation project: the beginning of a strategy plan design or implementation, the awarding of a grant, the start of a school year.

We seek arbitrary starting points for the 'hard work' of innovating. Here is a novel thought that is rather harder to slot into your iCal or Outlook calendar: a good starting block for an innovation team is right in the here-and-now.

Most successful innovators in and outside education spend their time always seeking out what doesn't quite work, what doesn't satisfy the needs of the people it should do, what could be made incrementally better.

They are not negative people; far from it, in fact, as they seek not to moan but make the world a better place, one incremental change at a time. Doing this means that they spend time – small snippets and extended periods, depending on what time they have available – looking at the world around them with a critical eye and an endless run of questions about why things are the way they are.

They are not satisfied to leave an under-par situation – they want to make it better as soon as possible.

What are things really like at the moment? If we were to take a snapshot in time, where is our school, where are our learners? What are people trying to achieve at the moment, and are they managing it? What are the areas where people find they're held back, or encouraged to take their learning further? How do we engage with parents, the school board, the wider community? How do we know they're happy with it? Where are the people who are happy with what we do? Where are the people who we don't know are either satisfied or not? What about the people who are not, at the moment, part of our school community? Why are they not? What are they doing instead?

This is a non-exhaustive list of questions that might be of interest to any innovator, and to answer any or all of these questions would take a long time, but that active immersion into the way things are needs to happen all the time.

Immersion is just as it sounds: long, deep and sometimes painful. The swimming pool analogy isn't bad for explaining it: If you were immersed in a swimming pool you'd have the water over your head. You would, over time, become short of breath. A real immersive experience would push that feeling just a little beyond what feels comfortable before, finally, at the last possible moment, coming up for breath. And, with every time you get immersed in the water, the longer you can bear it before coming up for breath.

With more practice, you can swim while holding your breath, travelling while building resistance to the pressure. In a school, this is the equivalent of the Head Teacher and other leaders being capable of not only managing business-as-usual, but also having the mental bandwidth, the practice of longitudinal immersion, to see potential for 'new innovation' as it arises.

How To Come Up With Great Ideas and Actually Make Them Happen

In short, it's about taking time to reflect, not regularly but constantly, on how things might be made better.

The best example of this ever-watchful, ever-improving 'formative assessment' for innovation in business is arguably Richard Branson, and the legions of entrepreneurs and business people who have modeled their behaviour on his.

When Richard Branson launched Virgin Atlantic, his airline, he had one rented plane and had decided to take on the behemoth British Airways on operating the London-US routes. He had sold up his baby – Virgin Records – for £1bn, crying his way down the pavement after the monumental deal. The cash was going to go straight into the cash-swallowing loss that was his new airline company.

It was a David and Goliath moment. At this point, most school leaders would have a lump of fear in their throat – selling the family silverware to fund a losing business sounds crazy.

However, contrary to what one might think, it was not a decision that would sink his Virgin empire if things went wrong: the leasing he could afford for eighteen months before throwing in the towel if, indeed, this David were to be pounded into the ground by British Airways' Goliath.

Of course, we know that Virgin has not only successfully taken on British Airways but has filled the space of several American carriers too, names now long gone. It's not done this based purely on the putsch of the launch of Virgin Atlantic thirty years ago – the launch of an innovation isn't enough to call something 'innovative' and then carry on as we always have done.

Rather than resting on his laurels, Branson, perceived as ever the optimist, spends most of his time seeking out the parts that don't work.

He spends most of his time in the First Horizon of the status quo, trying to work out what elements need tweaking to get the whole organisation to the Third Horizon of high innovation.

He does not spend his time solely dreaming about what that next Third Horizon might be.

A useful metaphor here might be that of a photographer with a telephoto lens: Branson zooms in constantly to see the detail and, between each shot, zooms out again to see the larger picture and how that detail fits in. Gathering those shots, gathering that evidence, requires a toolset beyond good questioning.

IMMERSION: GATHERING THE EVIDENCE

So when Richard Branson zooms in on the detail, what is it he is actually doing?

He spends time in the aircraft, in every class, taking the same journeys as the people paying him for the same thing.

He listens to cabin crew as much, if not more than his leadership teams.

He enters into conversations, and really listens to what customers say, with a view to using that feedback to change the way things work. He doesn't defend anything that doesn't work, or is perceived as not working: he writes it down and does something about it.

He encourages his other leaders to do the same, and considers every member of staff a leader – if air cabin crew get in touch with something that doesn't work, he helps pull the strings for it to be changed.

He writes everything down, to deal with it later, when he can. These are all small things, but his £1bn bet depended on it. The organisation's future depends on it for providing ever-better service on the customer-facing side, and on the employee-facing side it creates an empowering working environment of which staff are proud.

In schools, leaders might and do say they do all of these active observations: I walk the corridors, I visit classrooms, I meet parents (when their child has been naughty), I speak to the children and staff. But colleagues and students can often be left wondering if, when and by whom the crucial 'next action' will be taken.

The leader has certainly heard or seen, but has he or she really listened and watched, noted it down, shared it widely with those who can make the change, and then made sure that something is done about it?

And, in fact, many discussions about potential innovation in schools take place in meetings which have been set aside specifically to look at the issue, or occur as one point on an agenda of other administration chores and 'important' things to be done. Only certain people get invited – it's rare to have the whole school involved – meaning that groups can sometimes feel that they lack the credibility to come to decisions on issues that affect the whole school, the very issues that are probably most worth solving.

We've all been there: people arrive late as they have other 'urgent' things that needed sorting out first, they have not read the background context so they don't know where the need has come from, the idea to solve the problem is on your colleagues' lips before you've even described the problem.

Meetings of peers sitting around a table lead rarely lead to collaborative action towards solving a problem. Not everyone in the meeting is up to the same speed on the context of every issue.

Meeting agendas encourage us to deal with matters there and then, instead of simply exploring. And in an immersion into the First Horizon, trying to better understand the field in which we currently operate, simply exploring and making an effort not to come to any conclusions is the name of the game. 'Listening mode' is challenging to achieve, too: people are often occupied with thinking through their own response to others' ideas in the fast-paced desire to get to a conclusion as quickly as possible.

For the purpose of immersion, it is important that everyone understands the 'rules of the game', that this is more longitudinal than just one or two meetings, a process through which they can all be engaged with the use of some simple tools.

Many schools are afraid of involving such a wide range of people in an initial scoping of the current state of play, fearful sometimes that this will be a 'random' way of designing future strategy. Others still have already invested significant energy in designing school strategy or a vision statement, and feel that 'the work has been done already'.

That's as maybe, but the purpose of undertaking a period of immersion is to provide a snapshot in time on where you're at in achieving that vision. It can happen weeks after the vision has been decided, or years. Depending on how well the vision is interpreted and how tangible the evidence has been on the impact of its implementation, the length of time it takes to undertake a fresh immersion, and the new needs it uncovers, will be different.

Immersion in this First Horizon is also an essential step to come back to regularly, as a means of testing the assumptions behind the work we're currently doing. Most strategy and learning operates firmly in the realm of knowledge and reflection on what we know. Existing actions are often based on known knowns (the things we do and don't do, purposefully) and the known unknowns (things we're aware we're not doing and don't know but don't feel as being relevant to what we're undertaking currently). A deep immersion harnessing some of the techniques to follow will help us discover unknown unknowns, which may or may not be critical to improving the way we do things.

Observation is but one strategy for gathering evidence of existing challenges, or gaining insights into what innovative ideas we might develop next. There is a battery of immersion tools we can employ to gain as full a picture as possible, some of which we can do pretty much all the time, others which are better programmed in over a shorter period of time.

STORING WHAT YOU OBSERVE AND EXPERIENCE

We need a space in which to gather the evidence, as we go, until we make the time to do something with it. Often, the small thing you notice today as 'interesting' doesn't emerge as part of a problem until days, weeks or months later, when you make a connection with something else that's not quite working the way it should.

Schools are places where the god of 'tidying up' is one we worship almost every hour, on the hour. On her visits to schools in England, Australian educator Esme Capp had been surprised by the way everything was packed up at the end of each day: 'I'd say, leave it there! The goal is these children come back tomorrow, they revisit, they build, and they go deeper into the project.'

For her, classroom displays are not mere decoration or even celebration, but a vital part of the process of making learning visible, both to the children and to their teachers and parents.

The same is true for teams trying to be innovative: in order to think like a designer about our challenges we need to see the evidence of those emerging challenges all around us.

We mustn't tidy up; au contraire, we need to keep the evidence of our learning around us.

Bug Lists and Ideas Wallets

One simple routine is the act of keeping a 'bug list', a personal note of things you notice that just don't work as well as they could do: they have bugs that need ironing out.

You may not be able to iron them out just yet, or do it alone, but noting them down for a future problem-solving session is the first step. Problem-finding in this way, and keeping a record of all the problems one finds, allows us to prioritise those problems later, and solve them faster.

An 'ideas wallet' is another way to capture inspiration as it comes to you. Often we have creative ideas on the spur of the moment, when we least expect them, and often at times when we are not at work. Most of them get forgotten, many get written off by the time we get back to the workplace where we might be able to do something with them.

An ideas wallet acts as a creativity safety net of sorts: by noting the ideas down there and then, as they appear, we can't delete them prematurely, forget them, or write them off as unfeasible. Instead, we can continue to gather them, spot connections between them, attach them to needs identified in our bug list, and work with others who might be able to make them become a reality.

Learning Nests

My colleague Tom Barrett is a purveyor of 'learning nests', those physical, digital, large and pocket-sized spaces where observations and ideas can be nestled away until the moment where he, his team or the team that could do something about it have the mental bandwidth to go full force into solving the problem. His battery of techniques is borrowed from the creative industries and from his personal learning habits.

What sounds like 'taking notes' is something much more than that, as people are quick to recognise when Tom walks into a meeting with school leaders: on the production of a dog-eared Moleskine, and not a shiny tablet device.

The remark is often made as to how low-tech a way this is to record reflections, in an age when most meetings are dominated by the shield of the laptop lid. Tom explains his reasonings:

One of the challenges of being able to record an event or to take notes during a meeting is to be present with the people around you as much as possible, especially in the early occasions when you're working with them. So I tend to write things down in a notebook, which I find less invasive than a laptop, for example, or fumbling about with technology. I find it gives me greater freedom to get down quickly what I want to record, in sketches, notes, diagrams, whatever.

I tend to have a mixture of ways to record things. I think there's always a balance to be struck with these things. I have notebooks with handwritten notes which I tend to then transcribe. Some of those notes might go into a to-do list, for example. I'm always looking for digital spaces that work across the different platforms I use. Evernote works really well for me, because I can record all sorts of different things in it: handwritten notes, audio, movies, links, whatever I need, and it works on my phone as much as on the laptop.

I think that one of the reasons I don't just throw my paper notes out is that the actual paper tends to give me a great sense of context in which it was recorded. When you're making notes in a computer, on a Google Document or Evernote file, it tends to lack some of the idiosyncrasy of that particular moment in time. So looking back in a notebook you can see the coffee mug stains and the type of pen I used, and the scribbles that are generally much more specific and contextual. It's much less banal than just typing something in. Even though I might transpose some of my handwritten stuff into a digital space, I make sure I do keep those notebooks to give me a clearer sense of the story of those particular moments in time.

This process of committing in paper form, digitising some, but retaining the paper copies might feel very un-twenty-first century, inefficient even, but keeping those paper elements is important for Tom and other creatives. Often, creative teams trying to innovate will also take resources that were originally digital and turn them into physical printouts. Tom continues:

> *There are a couple of reasons why we might be conscious of making something into a physical artefact. One of them is how accessible that it is to other people. I could type something up but it might just stay on my computer, filed away out of sight. An idea written out like that doesn't necessarily lead to people understanding its context, either. Being able to create something physical is much more immediate, real, visceral to somebody, and helps them understand a new idea. When the idea is more than a short essay – for example, a drawing, photograph, sketch – they can see it, feel it, hold onto it, turn it around in their hands. Generally if you can physically walk around an idea then you're going to be able to have a clearer sense of what that idea is, literally turning it over in your mind as well.*
>
> *The other plus is just the flexibility of working physically. You're less constrained to a particular medium and one thing that we are restricted to with the technology is making something very very quickly typically involves writing it out.*
>
> *When we stray too far into describing things in that way it becomes harder for people to become flexible with their ideas. I think that idea, when we talk about prototyping something quickly, does so much to communicate that idea in a very quick way.*

John Kolko, the designer, puts it this way, referring to research from the realm of abductive thinking:

> *By taking the data out of the cognitive realm (the head), removing it from the digital realm (the computer), and making it tangible in the physical realm in one cohesive visual structure (the wall), the designer is freed of the natural memory limitations of the brain and the artificial organizational limitations of technology. Content can now be freely moved and manipulated, and the entire set of data can be seen at one time.*
>
> *Implicit and hidden meanings are uncovered by relating otherwise discrete chunks of data to one another, and*

positioning these chunks in the context of human behavior.

Google Ventures believe so strongly in getting ideas out there to make headways in technology projects that they invest in creating small, agile and relatively cheap 'War Rooms'.

These spaces are dedicated to one particular project during a 'sprint', a fast-paced burst of activity to make significant inroads to a project, or to overcome a particularly troublesome problem.

Getting ideas out of the head and onto paper or whiteboard is not, for Jake Knapp, the Google Ventures Partner, solely about the brain science that shows us it's effective. It's also about democratising the decision-making process, making sure that everyone who wants to be part of a project can quickly be on the same page. There's nobody guarding information for themselves – to do so puts you in the minority and at a disadvantage when everyone else is making decisions with ample data at their fingertips.

Building a project nest is a developmental process, not something that has boundaries. It is added to incrementally and over the course of a project. For example, throughout our work with a large luxury fashion brand in London we built small display cases of ideas for student design teams to use. These project nests then grew with the new material discovered by teams through their interviews, research and observations.

In the final showcase, weeks later, the project nest shows staff 'assessors' of ideas where those ideas came from, where the information was discovered and reveals the research skills of the student or participant in the process. They also show the dead ideas, the ones that didn't make the cut, and the journey the ideas took to end up as the innovation before them.

The advantage of having a physical space that shows the thinking journey behind the innovation isn't just one of self-justification; it also offers those coming to the innovation towards the end of the process the opportunity to be part of its continuing design, to play catchup with the research, the thinking and design process.

The 'new innovation' isn't so shiny or produced as to be either love or loathe in the eyes of those who might have to use it. The messiness of the learning nest provides visible hope that there is still scope for contribution and improvement – decisions have not yet been made on what is important, which remarks belong with each other.

I'd love to see school reception area walls coated with the thinking that has led to the innovations in learning and policy to which parents, students and the wider community can still have a chance to contribute. For the schools we work with they do indeed dedicate a wall space that becomes a working wall.

In many of the primary schools with whom we work in South Brisbane, Australia, the students have a whole room dedicated to the artefacts of their project. Whichever way you decide to do it, the fact that there is a messy learning space that learners or members of a team can contribute to, provides an ongoing support to project work.

This visible approach to showing thinking, not finished 'glossy' innovations, works with even your youngest learners. Nami Kim at American School in Japan Early Learning Center, Tokyo, has her youngest kindergarteners create their own 'frames' in which their learning journey can be posted, by them, as they feel they've learned something and want to show it. If kindergarteners can show how they're working out the world around them through this process, then so can school leaders.

You might also think about creating a teacher-based project nest throughout a semester or school year for all staff to collect, share and group their teaching and learning strategies. Kathleen McLean and colleagues at Mother Theresa Ormeau Primary School, south of Brisbane, Australia, have done exactly that. The original idea for their 'Visible Learning Nest' came about from a need to introduce new teachers to design thinking, a process the school had been using as a framework for learning since 2011.But with a large number of new teachers entering the school in 2013, the question was raised: How might we create a culture of reflection and develop common practices amongst all staff in design thinking?

Many staff members expressed a preference for a concrete, rather than digital space to access information, resources, ideas and examples as they would be easier to find and use. Given the busy nature of a new school with new staff, Kathleen noticed that it took a few terms to take off.

The first major contribution to a pool of expertise and experience was on the theme of developing this culture of reflection throughout all classes. The product of the teacher's thinking was a game plan, which mapped out some steps to successfully creating a culture of reflection using keywords as prompts, reflection routines, emotional learning strategies and a protocol for running peer critique sessions. It was briefly shared with all the staff at the next staff meeting:

> *In the following week a few members of the staff team added more strategies, tools, templates to the wall. At the beginning of the following term, all the members of staff were happy to be able to pull items directly from the wall and use them. It created some conversation around items that were added or which seemed to stay on the wall – it was all great progress.*
>
> *Yet, as the term progressed, it seemed that the wall was become underused and felt owned by only a few staff members.*

In response to this, staff were approached for a specific type of feedback the team had been working on – feedforward, or feedback that serves to provide ideas on resolving the problem. It was clear that the physical space had become overwhelming for many as items were added without explanation, context or identification, and the school focus had meanwhile shifted to other aspects of teaching and learning. As a result of this feedforward process, the wall was reorganised to help teachers make connections with its content. New labels were added to the wall to help teachers identify and follow as new items were added to the wall. When discussing ideas for teaching and learning, teachers were referred to items and examples on the wall to help reorientate them. Kathleen continues:

The other challenge facing us – the lack of group ownership over the wall – was met by rethinking how all staff might have a role in bringing ideas together, rather than just a select few who self-nominate. All the staff have said that it was a very valuable space and that they would like to create another space this year. But perhaps we'll take a new, guided, encouraged and more organised approach. The tools used and location would also be revised to ensure maximum engagement.

Gathering that evidence is one part. Doing something about it is quite another.

INTERVIEWS

To get around 'meetingitis', the disease of endless calendar invitations, schools often make use of 'staff surveys', particularly at times when larger strategy documents need pulling together.

These are only as successful at getting the right kind of information as the questions asked, and the order in which they are posed. They don't take account of the reactions of respondents, in real time, in the same way that a good interview and interviewer can do.

Having staff, students and parents understand the power of the interview as a tool to understand the status quo of the First Horizon is a great start. Interviews are different from those discussions we've experienced in meetings:

The interviewer asks his or her question and then only has one job: to listen to the response without interrupting;

- The contribution of the interviewee is recorded somewhere so it can be reviewed, compared and contrasted later.
- Good interviews ask questions about specific moments, and aim to get stories, not answers, out of the interviewee. Consider starting your interviews with questions about those specific moments: 'Tell me about the last time you...'
- Once people have revealed a problem in the interview, don't do what we tend to do in meetings and conversations (run over it with an unrelated question or remark): build on it. A simple way is to ask 'Why?', digging deeper into the perceived reasons for something happening. You might want to also review this later, and add your own gut feel as to why, and see if they match or contrast.
- What people say and what you have observed them doing are sometimes at odds with each other – dig deeper to find out the interesting root causes behind that inconsistency.
- Don't answer your own question before asking it. Let people take time before answering and don't rush to rephrase your question with your own example, as you'll sway their original (true) answer.
- Ask short, open-ended, neutral questions. 'Yes' is not a helpful answer, and means you haven't discussed the potential of the 'No' that makes up the other, interesting half of the story the person is yet to tell.
- Before you start an interview, there is clearly an advantage to writing down your first questions to get you started in a good direction. For example: What was it like the last time you saw...? Why would

someone else think that x or y might be better? How does x compare with y? What would the reply be to someone who says...? What does it feel like? What does it look like? Describe a moment where...

- In an interview itself, the order of questions being asked is hugely influential for the result you gain. We have to strike a balance between getting all the information we think we have needed in advance versus what emerges as the interviewer listens to the responses being given and wants to dig deeper. Often our first interview asks some questions in a set order, but then we allocate time for a second interview, often immediately after the first, where we dig deeper into specific insights or needs we've perceived in the interviewee's initial responses. The thing to avoid is forgetting to go back to those deeper questions, or going deep but then forgetting to back through the other questions we had decided were important to ask in the first place.

TOOLS FOR RECORDING INTERVIEWS

The tools we use to record interviews are important, too. If there is just one interviewer who is also there to record answers, then an audio recorder can be helpful, but has two downsides: first, the interviewee may not be quite so forthcoming on sighting the recording device; second, the interviewer may forget what those insights or needs were into which he or she wanted to dig deeper in a second phase of the interview.

If the interviewer can write notes on what he or she is hearing in real time, so much the better. Better still is to have an interviewer assistant who can scribe everything being said.

It is important to capture everything, as we can often find the great needs to meet or insights to be exploited in those throwaway remarks, in those apparently unimportant off-the-cuff stories.

The linearity of question-asking can get in the way of the flow of an interview, if set questions that need to be asked are simply listed in a bullet-point form, as above, or computer entry form to be filled out.

Paul J Corney was a customer seeking a new cell phone, and recounts two very different interviews undertaken in cell phone stores, leading to two very different outcomes.

In the first store, the employee asked for the information required for a new cell phone, using his computer form to gain it:

> *He was behind a counter and his computer screen was a barrier as was the counter we were sitting at. In a different store, the approach was less 'them and us', and the resulting interview a much more impactful one:*
>
> *Every piece of detail the salesman needs to form an opinion about you is there but the overlapping circles are not at all threatening or official. It mixes informality with the need for capture... Here's the twist: the salesman can choose which question to pose and when, depending on his assessment of the person sitting in front of him and their answers to some of the questions.*
>
> *It has 'doodle' space so it feels like a document that is purely for taking notes when actually it is the basis on which their document of record is created.*

The salesman Corney talks to points out that this form allows for the customer interview to be conducted at a pace that suits the customer and explore the issues that they want to discuss most first.

It makes the interview process easier, and more complete, putting the customer more at ease than the sequential form. Corney then goes on to provide some reasons why this graphical organiser is so much more successful for gathering information than a sequential form of interview:

- It's co-created: it feels like a sketch you both draw up.
- It's informal: it encourages interviewer and interviewee to scribble – it doesn't feel like it's an official record that we 'have to get right'.
- It's personal: 'It's all about u' is the title, and that's how it comes across.
- It models structured flexibility: it's an interview spine that, in the hands of good interviewers (which is what successful sales people are), provides an insight into a prospective client's needs against which they can pitch a product. Similarly, for a learning organisation looking to innovate, interviews like this provide the insight required to suggest what innovations might need to be created later.
- It's a neutral object: we focus on filling in the worksheet not the system – it's a neutral space.

Much of these traits extends to the use of blank, folded A3 sheets of paper that we use in our own immersion workshops, where there is a degree of formality (a folded page per participant being interviewed, and some guiding questions on a board) but the freedom to dive deep into the issues being raised by the interviewee.

Corney continues: 'Today reminded me that successfully capturing information and knowledge is very much dependent on the way you go about it. It reinforced the need for good tools and techniques and people well versed in using them and seeing the value in them.'

Those skills in using interview techniques cannot be left to chance, or to one's perceptions of what makes a successful interview. They need to be taught, practised before being put into action to create something as important and potentially long term as a school strategy.

At the Stanford University d.school, students explore

how new products and services might be created through interviews, trying to gain a sense of empathy for those who will benefit from certain problems being solved.

The school provide some rules of thumb about interviewing that fit well within the cadre of a school improvement immersion:

- Look for inconsistencies. Sometimes what people say and what they do are different. These inconsistencies often hide interesting insights.
- Don't be afraid of silence. Interviewers often feel the need to ask another question when there is a pause. If you allow for silence, a person can reflect on what they've just said and may reveal something deeper.
- Don't suggest answers to your questions. Even if they pause before answering, don't help them by suggesting an answer. This can unintentionally get people to say things that agree with your expectations.
- Ask questions neutrally. 'What do you think about this idea?' is a better question than 'Don't you think this idea is great?' because the first question doesn't imply that there is a right answer.
- Don't ask binary questions. Binary questions can be answered in a word; you want to host a conversation built upon stories.
- Only ask one question at a time, one person at a time. Resist the urge to ambush your user.

THE FIVE WHYS
One such interview technique is The Five Whys. The technique was developed as a systematic problem-solving tool by Taiichi Ohno, the creator of the Toyota Production System that helped Japanese auto manufacturing take on America's 'big three'.

The system, dubbed 'lean manufacturing', cut out extraneous bureaucracy when it came to problem-finding and empowered anyone on the production to line to stop the entire line in order to solve a problem they had spotted. It was therefore paramount that all production assembly line workers were mentally equipped with problem-finding skills.

Since then, it has evolved to become a stalwart of technology startups trying to find profound problems they can design websites or apps to solve. But the technique has been particularly useful in the medical field too, with Britain's National Health Service departments using it to get to the root problems that reduce in-hospital infection rates or improving patient care.

For example, if patients experience delays in getting to theatre, it can cause knock-on effects for others awaiting surgery, or even delay the surgery to another day altogether if the surgeons involved will be stretched beyond acceptable working hours.

Understanding why patients are late to surgery is not as simple as blaming the porters. Using the five whys, a different explanation might arise. Here is an example offered by the NHS itself to its own staff:

The patient was late in theatre, it caused a delay. Why?
There was a long wait for a trolley. Why?
A replacement trolley had to be found. Why?
The original trolley's safety rail was worn and had eventually broken. Why?
It had not been regularly checked for wear. Why?

The root cause - there is no equipment maintenance schedule. Setting up a proper maintenance schedule helps ensure that patients should never again be late due to faulty equipment. This reduces delays and improves flow. If you simply repair the trolley or do a one-off safety rail check, the problem may happen again sometime in the future.

In another example, the diagnosis of a cancer is delayed,

leading to a nervous wait and, potentially, a worse prognosis:

> *The patient's diagnosis of skin cancer was considerably delayed. Why?*
> *The excision biopsy report was not seen by the surgeon. Why?*
> *The report was filed in the patient's notes without being seen by the surgeon. Why?*
> *It was the receptionist job to do the filing. Why?*
> *The junior doctors were busy with other tasks. Why?*
> *The root cause - that the doctors' other tasks were seen as more important than filing. The system has now been changed. A copy of all biopsy reports is now sent to the consultant surgeon responsible for the patient and no reports are filed unless they have been signed by a doctor.*

Schools and other learning organisations with whom we've used this technique can find it useful. 'Students in Form 2F are misbehaving in class' can be down to different root causes depending on so many factors, so an individual teacher can use this for themselves to identify what actions they might take personally, or whom they might ask for help in resolving the issue, while a school leadership team asking the same five whys on the same topic will end up with a different set of actions they could undertake to solve the issue.

THE SQUID
The Squid is another means through which to learn about an organisation, best undertaken with three or four people around a large wall space. Starting with a broad challenge that people are looking at (misbehaviour; student-led learning; healthy eating...), each person around the wall privately asks one question, writing it on a post-it note, and then all three or four questions are posted up at once.

Then, altogether, the team set about providing any possible answers to each question. This means that the first round of answers could be as few as three, or as many as a dozen, for example. Only once all the questions have been answered as exhaustively as the group feels necessary can the whole group then move on to pose one more question about each of those answers.

Now, the meaning behind 'the Squid' becomes clear: tentacles of questions and answers will stretch across the wall until such a time that the exercise is deemed finished – perhaps within five questions' worth of Q&A.

Each answer contributes towards the immersion of the larger project or strategy we are developing. By the end of the process, there may be some great insights that begin to provide answers for some of the challenges the organisation is currently facing.

SKETCHING AND PHOTOGRAPHING

Interviews or a structured discussion activity are hugely powerful, particularly so when you can rely upon an independent scribe to get everything down, and not to editorialise, purposefully or by accident.

But words are words, and can still leave much to interpretation. So, an immersion has to be more than just 'taking my word for it'. Ideally, you can capture the actual words, observe the actual actions of those people who stand to benefit from a new strategy or vision.

Even the most technophobic Director or Chief Executive has a device that can capture audio, photographs and/or video.

These tools allow large teams to capture more 'real' data than ever before, rather than simply relying on hearsay, supposition or guesswork.

Audio
Just recording some audio using a voice memo app on a smartphone is an incredibly powerful means of communicating a need.

People tend to speak much more openly about the

problems and challenges affecting them in daily life when there is not a film camera stuck in front of their face.

A surreptitious audio recording, with their permission, takes barely minutes of conversation before the audio recorder, or phone, is forgotten about, and the truth is out.

It is important to get permission from people before recording them, in audio, photograph or video, as you never know if you'll need their firsthand testimony to make a case further down the road, in a more public forum.

Sure, the decision-making process might be between a smaller group, but there is always the opportunity when you do have permission to make a much stronger case for your eventual ideas and prototypes when you have evidence like this to back you up.

Video
It can be tempting to record people in video. There are a few advantages to this if you want to use the material later in a pitch presentation, for example, to explain and justify your eventual ideas.

However, to record good video you also need good audio. Recording a talking head type conversation on a mobile phone video will have audio that is too poor to make a good case. Recording it on a proper film camera with separate audio recording will sound great, but it will take a lot more time to pull together the final clip.

Above all, there are consequences for the type of testimonial you will get – people say different things with a pro camera in front of them than they do when it's 'just a quiet conversation'.

Photographs
Photos can be super for quickly grabbing evidence of things that don't work, or which people habitually use in the wrong way. A series of photos of different people who

enter a school and look confused as they seek the reception desk is a powerful message that things might need to change.

Photos are easy to edit, to render your subjects anonymous and then use the evidence of a problem in a public setting. You could also go to the trouble of seeking permission after the fact, if you required it.

One proviso with photos: we can sometimes snap a general scene and not be aware of the element we need to observe – we look without seeing.

Pay attention so as not to see everything down a viewfinder, but to look up and observe the world with your naked eye too. It's a different set of clues that you will receive.

Sketching
Sketching is perhaps more powerful than photography in many ways, even if it takes a few seconds or minutes more.

When we sketch, we're editorialising to a degree in that we choose what to draw – a photograph can accidentally take things in that we can analyse later, whereas when we sketch we have to make those decisions there and then.

But that very act of choosing makes us observe more closely. In one school, where architects were seeking inspiration for their redesign, students had used walking tours to see their school and look for improvements. The results were fairly traditional plans for a new school.

But when we took the same students around with a sketch book, the results were different. They editorialised. They observed, didn't just look. They saw things they hadn't really internalised before.

For example, students never seemed to lock their lockers – the locks were always made to look closed, but they were left open. The students invented a new word – flocking (false locking) – to describe the phenomenon.

With that as inspiration, they began to observe, to seek out, any other clues around safety and security that could help redesign things for the better later on.

Another team at the same school observed the furniture layouts of the school, sketching only five different compositions of desks and chairs throughout the whole K-12 institution. And yet, where the school had attempted a prototype space with soft furnishings and relaxed areas, students sketched their peers falling asleep in the comfort.

Other students wondered whether technology was working well. They noticed that, with the lid of laptop computers obscuring much of the eye contact of students, those who used only their mobile phones communicated a lot more about their work, and only referred intermittently to their phones to check up on a specific piece of information.

Genchi Genbutsu

The Japanese term for this kind of active observation, rather than just presupposing or 'looking, not seeing', is called Genchi Genbutsu. It literally means: get out and see for yourself.

Toyota are arguably the Japanese grandmasters of this technique, led by the founder of their world-famous manufacturing system, Taiichi Ohno, and it forms part of their formal five-part strategy for working.

They describe it thus: The best practice is to go and see the location or process where the problem exists in order to solve that problem more quickly and efficiently. To grasp problems, confirm the facts and analyse root causes.

The Toyota Production System requires a high level of management presence on the factory floor, so that if a problem exists in this area it should be first of all correctly understood before being solved.

In Jeffrey Liker's *The Toyota Way* we see the notion taken beyond the factory floor.

Yuji Yokoya was the chief engineer for the 2004 Toyota Sienna redesign. Yokoya had never worked on a car made for the North American market, and he felt the need to practise some Genchi Genbutsu and get out to North America to gain some sense of empathy for a North American driver, and the potential purchaser of this new car.

In the end, Yokoya drove a previous model Sienna throughout all 50 American states as well as all 13 provinces and territories of Canada. He got as far as the streets of Mexico.

Why was such a costly and timely roadtrip necessary? Was this the midlife crisis of a successful engineer, or a genius move to make major changes to an otherwise successful (in the Japanese market) car?

What he learned could not have been learned from any analytical data, survey or web search. Why? Because the things he observed needed observing by a Japanese Toyota engineer to make sense – they needed that empathetic, but foreign eye, to be seen afresh.

For example, he discovered that roads in Canada are very different from those in the US – they have a very high central reservation designed to deal with the never-ending snowfall of winter. He learned that the winds in Mississippi are so strong at times that, if the family-sized Sienna were not designed with this in mind, it might have flipped over with the force.

The most valuable lesson was perhaps to do with a tiny, non-engineering type problem: cup holders. In his native Japan people rarely eat or drink in their vehicles, while their North American counterparts were relatively settled in the habit of eating several of their daily meals within the car, on the move.

From the many design and engineering problems he spotted, Yokoya's team developed a new Sienna for 2004, equipped with 14 cup holders and a flip tray specifically designed for your Big Mac and fries. It was their best-selling model yet. The notion of 'getting out there and seeing it' might well seem like a drawback for leadership teams looking after large institutions, or entire districts, states or countries.

We can't all afford 50-state road trips to get a firsthand insight. To undertake an extensive immersion, in person, 'out there' might not be possible. But it's less about the physical act than the mental mindset. Toyota explain further:

The nature of the phrase is less about the physical act of visiting a site but more to do with a personal understanding of the full implications of any action within an environment as a whole. The impact of changing one's mindset, often by applying a strong sense of empathy to how others might view a situation, is powerful.

Even in a workshop type situation, normally within the air-conditioned magnolia of a plush hotel or a school meeting room with no wifi (and no connection to the outside world), the mindset change put in place by considering every actor's feelings and potential observations of the current situation is profound.

From one workshop in a business centre in Spain looking at problems in schools 500 miles away: 'This workshop focused on people and used real examples; the process was involving.' From a Headteacher in England: 'The fact that everyone can take part and feels a necessity to join in means that all views, good and bad are taken into account.' From a team in Australia looking at a perennial challenge they hadn't (yet) overcome: 'We loved having the time to explore ideas, good and bad, without negativity, to see things from so many perspectives.'

Just making an effort to connect with people from other perspectives transforms our thinking about what the underlying challenges we need to address might be. This immersion process of the First Horizon requires a mindset, too, where one holds one's ideas lightly.

Even this early on, many people have already developed an idea of what they think the solution to the problem they think exists might be. That's a big pair of assumptions – that we know both the problem and solution. In an innovation incubator my firm helped develop with a school district in South Carolina, USA, we saw the difference between teams who had settled on an idea from the start versus those who had a flimsy idea and were prepared to test their assumptions through a deeper immersion than they had initially done, in order to generate tweaks to their existing ideas for solving problems they had identified.

Others still felt the need to overhaul their total idea, after seeing a totally different problem that needed solving more urgently.

For example, CrowdED was designed to replicate the kind of cash donation crowdsourcing for schools that one can see on a multitude of different sites, but do it locally – for local schools, with donations from local people. It was a good idea, but it didn't really think about the motivation of the people donating.

Do locals want to donate cash to their local schools, or do they want to donate something more valuable – their time, expertise, 'stuff'? And who were the people who would gain most from donating to a school? Parents? Kids themselves? Or local businesses? It needed the team to get out and speak to some of those potential business partners to realise that it wasn't cash, but time, expertise and products that they would be more than happy to donate to local schools for projects.

The idea didn't just pivot from cash donations – it took on a whole new ethic and drive. The teams who held their ideas lightly, as my colleague Tom Barrett would put it, and changed them based on their actual observations and empathy studies (or Genchi Genbutsu) ended up winning investment for their ideas. Those who had settled down too quickly on their idea failed to gain support for the ideas further down the line.

The mindset of Genchi Genbutsu creates a great shift in the way we approach innovation, by testing one's assumptions. We do this by visiting, physically or in our mind's eye, the people, places and situations with the specific goal of challenging our own assumptions.

Extreme Users
Something we also see in our stories of people changing, or pivoting, their ideas based on potential users' feedback, is a greater understanding of users that do not constitute 'normal', whatever that is. A mistake when we set out to observe the world around us is that we seek people like us, or we seek people for whom we think a problem exists, instead of looking holistically at all the groups who might be affected in our problem area.

For example, in the North of England we helped run a startup incubator, called The Difference Engine. Smart teams from across Europe participated in a fast-paced race to get investment.

One team had the bright idea of car sharing facilitated by their online service, something that had worked extremely well in their native Estonia. They had already found one extreme set of users – people in the UK who loved the idea. But transposed to the United Kingdom, even with a small group of enthusiasts at one extreme, they were finding it hard to develop the service.

The main reason? They hadn't spent time exploring the two other groups – people who hated the idea on one end and those who had never heard of it and wouldn't know if they needed it somewhere in the middle of this spectrum of extremes.

On the flip side, another company in the same incubator, ScreechTV, had an idea based on one extreme – sports fans in football stadia wanting to be entertained at halftime – but realised that the problem it was solving was actually with people on the other extreme, who watch football from home and get bored far quicker.

The firm has grown over the past three years and received countless rounds of multi-million dollar investment, offering additional entertainment through television screens that matches up with the event you are watching.

In schools and other education institutions, Extreme Users exist in every category. Speaking as a French teacher, there were those students who wanted to be French and those who had no intention of ever travelling beyond the city limits. There are teachers who live and love technology and those who, apparently, loathe it.

Despite the segmentation, Extreme Users make up the most worthwhile human element to explore in most problems worth solving.

Normally, human nature makes sure that we strive to avoid these people – they complain the most, they are the loudest, they are the squeaky wheels who get the oil. But they are also the ones who are least engaged, who care the least, who don't want to have anything to do with your innovative ideas, or even your institution. These are the Extreme Users, who make up both ends of the spectrum on which are nearly all of our users, or the people who will benefit from a new strategy and vision designed to solve problems and build on successes.

Practically, understanding these Extreme Users is best facilitated by the use of a Persona.

Bill Aulet describes how one might make up a Persona that actually serves a practical purpose in his book *Disciplined Entrepreneurship*:

> *Those with a marketing background are likely familiar with the concept of a Persona, using a generic name like Mary Marketing or Ollie Owner as a composite of what the marketing team thinks the typical customer is like...*
>
> *While even a generic Persona can be helpful, it is best to push the process even further. The Persona should be a real person, not a composite. By choosing an actual end user as your Persona, your Persona becomes concrete, leaving no room for second-guessing. Is your target customer happy with their region's education system?*

> ...
> *Does your target customer prefer a closed software ecosystem like throne the Apple iPhone provides, or an open ecosystem like the Android mobile operating system? Or does your target customer simply want to check email reliably on the go? You can debate these questions internally, but if your Persona is a real person, there is only one right answer.*

But he goes further, pointing out that no one Persona makes up 100% of the people who will benefit from your vision or innovation: No one end user represents 100 percent of the characteristics of every end user in your End User Profile. Bearing this in mind, it's much more useful to develop a couple of Personas, based around the two extremes of any given group you're aiming to engage with your innovation.

Drawing up Extreme Users with actual people in mind, while anonymising the end drawn out Persona nonetheless, means that the entire team will have a clear idea for whom the problem being investigated is most 'painful', for whom they might be designing an eventual vision or innovation.

The fact is, by solving the problem for them, you may well be solving it for many other people in the middle of the spectrum. In fact, the concept of designing for the extremes is something that has become law in some jurisdictions.

For example, in Norway, a certain percentage of public projects must be designed according to the principle of Universal Design, designing the solution to any given problem from the perspective of those with the least mobility, the least access to the service in the first place.

In Norway, Extreme Users form the basis of problem finding that leads to solutions that benefit everyone greatly. For example, when a beachside promenade is due to be rebuilt, it is redesigned from the perspective of wheelchair users first and foremost – wide enough for two chairs to pass, with beach access provided via flexible walkways that are easy for wheelchair users to access. As a result, mums with their push buggies also benefit, no longer having to wait in a nook while the rest of the world squeezes past.

When we make an effort to see the problem area we've chosen from the perspective of these Extreme Users, we gain insight into a multitude of smaller challenges: misconceptions, assumptions and problems for specific groups of people that may, and probably will, contribute towards a better solution further down the road.

NEXT STEPS IN IMMERSION AND GATHERING

Design Your Team

- ✓ Bring together an innovation design team who can represent a large array of those who populate your learning community.
- ✓ Spend some time with the innovation design team to explore the different mindsets of innovation. Do some people naturally fall into certain mindsets? Are there some activities they can undertake to experience the First Horizon from a different perspective?
- ✓ Start your own bug list and innovation wallet. Encourage your design team to do the same. Are there any small, manageable changes that can be made on an ongoing basis to improve the learner experience thanks to noticing the small things?
- ✓ Explore other tools for gathering information. Print them out as cards and make them available to the wider team, just as the Government Digital Service in the UK has done for the public.
- ✓ Look at your last long-term school plan. Did you achieve all the goals on it? Did it take five years to achieve them? Do the goals feel as relevant today as they did back then?
- ✓ What are the lowest financial cost ideas that people have wanted to develop but maybe been dissuaded from trying in the past? Make note of them for later, in case they meet the genuine needs that arise in the First Horizon.

Design Your 'Set'
- ✓ Set up a project nest where physical artefacts from

your immersion into the First Horizon can be placed.
- ✓ Make the wall or space as accessible as possible – especially to children, they need to feel they can contribute anything, any time.
- ✓ Encourage all sorts of contributions from those you work with, but do not group them too much – leave the synthesis until it feels the immersion phase is 'done'. Allow your wall space to be messy and jumbled to reflect the breadth of ideas and coverage in the first part of your topic. (Don't worry, you will organise it later on.)
- ✓ Plan for children, parents and teachers to have the opportunity to discuss what is displayed with their peers.
- ✓ Post screenshots of videos with a short bullet-point summary of the key points and a short URL (from a service such as bit.ly) and images from any events you've held on the innovation project as a reminder of those moments. Get the digital into the physical.
- ✓ Provide ample post-it notes and pens as a way to leave comments on other people's work.

Get Out There And Observe
- ✓ Interview and sketch a wide variety of actors going about their learning and work. Try to avoid framing a problem at the start – just observe, note everything down and put yourself in their shoes.
- ✓ Get out and about to see your organisation from as many different viewpoints and perspectives as possible.
- ✓ Who are your extreme users for different transactions and operations in the organisation? Can you draw them, and find their needs? Create a staffroom project nest where artefacts on teaching and learning can be collected, contributed, synthesised into clusters and shared on an ongoing basis.

THE FIRST HORIZON: PROBLEM FINDING

'Designers thrive on problem setting, at least as much as problem solving.'

Bill Buxton, principal researcher at Microsoft

Ewan McIntosh

SYNTHESIS: DEFINING YOUR PAIN

Having gathered a wide range of evidence, the process of synthesis kicks in. You know when it feels time to move on: the pace of contribution to the immersion takes a dip, the material gathered feels significant and 'worth' working with, and people may already have started to cluster things together, keen to make sense of what is already there.

Alternatively, if you're keeping an ideas wallet and bug list over time, you maybe schedule in a termly session to synthesise everyone's discoveries over that period.

Synthesis involves four key processes: gathering clusters of related material, spotting gaps, spotting opposites and defining problems that haven't been solved, or defining which opportunities need to be harnessed.

The process requires a shared space, the project nest, from the immersion phase. And as the synthesis process begins, you will find team members wanting to add additional information that they recall but have not yet committed, so a good supply of sticky notes, index cards with blu tac, and even a laptop and printer are good to have on hand.

The goal of the synthesis is to define the 'pains' experienced by current or potential members of your learning community. We talk about 'pains' as a way of conveying that, in learning communities more than many other environments, there will be a myriad of needs from the niggling to the immense: our challenge is to prioritise those needs that are really worth meeting, to resolve those needs that are indeed 'painful' for the learning community.

ARE YOU READY TO BRING IT ALL TOGETHER?

If your team members have been deep immersing themselves in conflicting, complex ideas for some time, there will come a point when it's essential to make sense of things. But in my experience, people often try to jump to this moment of synthesis too early: they haven't been immersed long enough, their experiences are not deep enough, or broad enough.

The team does not have as complete and holistic enough an understanding of the field in which they want to innovate. They may have already jumped to conclusions during the immersion phase as to the reasons behind what they are observing. By pointing out to people that this moment of reasoning and judging will come later, during a period of synthesis, it helps to keep them purely in observing and listening mode during immersion.

Nonetheless, it is possible that, after having started out on a synthesis of the facts, your team realises that it needs to go back and speak to more people, observe more of people's unthinking actions and capture more evidence of actual behaviour and needs.

The first signs that you need to go back to the immersion are often when people find themselves adding additional information to the project nest, using post-it notes, that isn't based on what was actually experienced but on conjecture. For example, in working with a not-for-profit on their strategy, the immersion phase revolved entirely around the teachers that it was there to serve, but did not provide much indication of the role played by sponsors and benefactors in making that work happen.

The conundrum to answer was: are the sponsors and benefactors at the core of redefining the next innovation of the organisation or not?

The only way to answer this was to go back and speak to more of those sponsors and benefactors, to see what needs emerged. The need to do this wasn't brought into focus until the point where we attempted to synthesise everything we had collectively discovered from our immersion.

ADDING WHAT YOU EXPERIENCE OR FEEL, BUT NOT WHAT YOU THINK OTHERS EXPERIENCE OR FEEL

There is nothing wrong at this stage with people adding their own gut feel, their own prior experiences and hypotheses about why they have felt a particular way. This is fine, provided it's based on what has actually happened to them.

What is confusing and contradictory, and generally unhelpful, is when people begin to hypothesise around what they think other people feel about an issue. Doing this shows that the team either needs to go back to the field and prove or disprove this gut feel or recognise that what they think is happening might not actually be the case.

For leaders, this is an easy trap to fall into, but imposing what you have 'always thought' as being the case when the actual deep immersion evidence shows something different negates the entire process.

Having a deep immersion confirm, though, what your gut has always told you adds a degree of urgency to drawing a conclusion as to what the underlying problem actually is.

RECALL AND REMEMBER

Before we can work out what the problem worth solving or ideas to develop next might be, we need to gather everything from the immersion phase that is not yet on the project nest, again making physical what people have seen online or have held in their memories up until now.

It is also an opportunity for team members to explain, through stories told, the meaning and significance behind their artefacts and brief post-it note handles. When adding additional observations, or if existing post-it note descriptions and artefacts are unclear, the team should try to clarify what was meant through concrete language. Vague, policy-type language is incredibly unhelpful as you try to define needs.

There are some perennials in 'education speak' that appear again and again. For example, post-it notes that say 'time' mean nothing.

When you hear the stories that led to 'time' being written on post-it notes the 'pains' of those people are so varied, and the stories make this vague word take on great meaning, revealing strong 'pains' that need to be solved. 'Time' could mean:

- 'I don't have enough time'
- 'I don't get predictable stretches of time to develop ideas'
- 'The time I have is at unproductive times of the day'
- 'All the development time I get is in chunks that

are too short to do anything worthwhile'
- 'The time I have is filled up with meetings by other people'
- 'The timetable tells me when to do my development work, but my brain tells me it's best done at 9pm'
- 'I don't have time free to develop ideas at the same time as my colleagues are free – we can't collaborate' 'Time zone differences make collaboration with schools in Australia / United States / China too difficult'

Recall is about taking what we've observed and heard in a process of immersion and teasing out what exactly is meant by the words used. From an ambiguous 'time' we end up with potentially endless definitions of what was actually meant.

So, during the immersion phase and, as we recall and remember, in synthesis, it is useful to have someone in your team who is responsible for querying language, making sure that concrete language is used. That means the actual words used by the person we interviewed or observed in immersion, or a clarification after the fact. This effort in clarity concerning what was heard and observed is a great help in honing down to what the core underlying problem might be.

CONNECT AND CLUSTER

In any deep stretches of thinking, we can all get muddled by the complexity of the ideas before us. It is a difficult mental task to work out what connects to what, which ideas are more outliers on their own and which concepts tie to the core of the challenge we're exploring. Linear thinking, where 'a' causes 'b' to happen, is great for textbook writers, but isn't the way the world works. How can we make sense of information in a way that also shows up the complex connections and sub-connections between ideas, concepts and facts?

The answer – hexagons, not squares. An effective tool for beginning to synthesise ideas is Hexagonal Thinking. Hexagons, rather than the squares or rectangles of the ubiquitous standard post-it note that you might associate with innovation projects, offer more sides with which to connect ideas. Each key concept that we can pull out of our recalled and remembered data can be summarised on a hexagonal post-it or card. The content behind each 'headline' needs to be specific enough for the team to quickly understand what is meant, but descriptive enough not to leave out the important details in the original cluster of material that led to the summary headline. Participants in the process then place the cards together in the way that makes most sense to them – some ideas will connect to up to five others, others will lie at the end of a long sequential order, others still will appear in small outlying positions, on their own. It's a great idea to try this as separate small pairings or groupings first, and then see where there is agreement or discord in the connections people are making. The technique was first pioneered in the oil and gas industry, and is highlighted in The Living Company, by the creator of 'the learning organisation' concept and Royal Dutch Shell, Arie de Geus.

De Geus had found that when he and executives were trying to help insurance people better understand their complex products, the expensive computer simulations they had developed were not doing the job: staff were too busy trying to 'win' the simulation that the more significant, and complex, information about the products was lost. With the introduction of hexagonal thinking, those complex connections were made swiftly and deeply. It has since been used in business as a means of tackling perennial 'wicked problems', a concept we'll explore in more depth later.

In schools, we've seen it put to use in the classroom by practitioners such as Chris Harte and David Didau. Harte, an educator based in Melbourne, Australia, uses the visual, tactical hexagons to help students see the complex connections between the various verb structures of the French language.

One of the teachers in a school with which my organisation works, Brisbane educator Elisabeth Hales, used a simple set of cards to help students home down on the key connections after a rich environmental immersion, as part of a design thinking project.

Quickly, students were able to model to one another their different takes on what they had experienced and researched – no two hexagonal syntheses were the same.

Even with our youngest learners, in a Juniors class in Sydney, teacher Anh Nguyen was able to record the thinking process and reasoning of children as they connect complex and abstract concepts together using this simple technique. Offering students the chance to verbalise, publicly, about why they have chosen a particular connection is vital for the process to have its biggest potential impact on thinking and learning. For those working on innovations, the connections that can be made are fascinating, too, showing the complex relationships between elements we have gathered in our First Horizon immersion and often revealing elements at the core of these relationships we hadn't spotted before.

DEFINING PROBLEMS THAT HAVEN'T BEEN SOLVED

The key to a great idea is finding a great problem to solve in the first place, and the richest ones for innovation are often labelled 'wicked problems':

1. The causes of the problem are not just complex but deeply ambiguous; you can tell why things are happening the way they are and what causes them to do so.

2. The problem doesn't fit neatly into any category you've encountered before; it looks and feels entirely unique, so the problem-solving approaches you've used in the past don't seem to apply.

3. Each attempt at devising a solution changes the understanding of the problem and how you think about it.

4. There is no clear stopping rule; it is difficult to tell when the problem is 'solved' and what that solution may look like when you reach it.

Such wicked problems outside the world of education often take on a socio-economic angle: solving the problems of drug or substance abuse, getting people out of the cycle of poverty, and so on. In schools, the problems are often less 'noble' sounding, but just as troublesome, open-ended, uncategorised and ambiguous as to their cause and effect.

For example, some schools appear to have always had a perennial littering problem, or graffiti is hard to stub out. 'Raising student attainment' or 'increasing parental engagement' might be others which are even more complex – we never know when we're done improving them.

These rough problem areas become evident early on, often during an initial immersion into something more general, or as a result of the same factors popping up time and time again in a bug list.

Having synthesised the evidence gathered in your immersion you will have already identified connections between different aspects of the way things are done at the moment, potential gaps in the way things are done, opportunities to create something different altogether, or opportunities to build on an outlying idea that has been ignored until now.

But knowing the rough problem area is not the same as defining the problem. To do that, we need to get more specific.

Three Powerful Words: How Might We...
Much has been written about these magical words. At the last count there were over 7.5m results for the Google search on 'How Might We', the 'secret phrase top innovators use' according to the Harvard Business Review. Why do these particular words free up creative space?

The 'how' part assumes there are solutions out there -- it provides creative confidence, Brown said to me. "'Might' says we can put ideas out there that might work or might not – either way, it's OK. And the 'we' part says we're going to do it together and build on each other's ideas."

In innovation workshops with entire faculty, it is tempting to have everyone looking to solve the same challenge – after all, that will bring a certain leadership in goal.

Yet, time after time, we see a benefit in splitting faculty into teams of 3-5 people to investigate a broad challenge area, in the form of a wicked problem, and see what different, more specific problems they unearth through their immersion and synthesis.

Even when faced with the same broad wicked problem to investigate, teams from the same school can develop wildly different specific problems that lend themselves well to being solved. For example, 'engaging better with the school community' is too broad, and doesn't help us really understand the problem at heart (that is, what is it we're trying to solve?).

But in the hands of some mixed-school teams in Australia, one wicked problem becomes a wide selection of far more precise, concrete How Might We problems which spur us better into ideation:

- How might we improve the attendance of our indigenous parents at parent-teacher interviews?
- How might we help get technologists to talk to teachers and teachers to talk to technologists?
- How might we better engage our parents with what we really do in our classrooms?
- How might we inform parents about what they need to know when they don't have internet access at home?
- How might we create mental space for teachers to get reengaged and experiment, be free to be more creative?
- How might we help parents understand that how we teach their kids needs to change?
- How might we help teachers to redefine their role as learners?
- How might we educate our parents to understand the educational benefits of an education grounded in real world mathematics?

An English elementary school, Simon de Senlis Primary School, was looking at ways to reinvigorate the beginning of its school year. From that broad exploratory area, their How Might We statements led to swift ideation and a raft of new challenging opportunities for young people:

> How might we ensure that children's return to school is motivating and exciting in order that they are emotionally and academically ready to achieve their full potential?
> How might we crack on in September?
> How might we help learning start on September 5th while easing in those children who need eased in?
> How might we help students on September 5th understand what a successful end to the year will look like?
> How might we involve parents in pitching sessions that engage all children?
> How might we help all students understand why they feel what they feel when they come back to school after the summer?
> How might we help all students adapt to change over summertime?

From one wicked problem sprouts a broad variety of small, concrete problems, but they are small enough to be ideated upon, and those ideas prototyped, by relatively small teams, without the need for heavyweight accord and agreement from senior leadership, school boards and so forth.

Each problem has been developed using a common set of experiences, insights, observations and data, but with a different empathetic lens. The difference this makes to problem definition is obvious, and yet another reason for leadership teams to beware defining problems from within the closets of the boardroom.

CONCRETE LANGUAGE EQUALS CONCRETE RESULTS

A short note on the choice of language in our How Might We problems.

You'll notice that the language is down-to-earth, often the opposite of the kind of visionary or strategy-type language we see in those five-year plans. This is more than accidental. It is by design. Teams don't get to that 'crunchy' language alone, but rather through each team critiquing each other's problem statements.

The use of Plain English helps make clear the problems we frame and the evidence that describes them.

As Lorena Sutherland, content lead for Office of the Public Guardian in the United Kingdom puts it, it's not dumbing down, but opening up the potential for people to engage with the idea.

There are some key questions and learning points that come around in each critique, which help form better, more actionable problem statements:

1. The How Might We statement appears to be offering an answer to the problem. Often we have to remove clauses that begin 'by -ing...'. For example: 'How might we get more parents to come to parent conferences by communicating better?' The fact is, better communication might not be the only, or the best, answer to this problem.

2. What exactly is the problem you're talking about? Sometimes, the How Might We statement covers up the underlying problem that we're trying to solve. The problem that has emerged through your intensive Immersion, Observation and Empathy activities has to be revealed somehow in the problem you're framing. An incredibly clear example of this was a rather general problem statement: 'How might we engage pupils better through PBL?'.

It's a lovely idea – Project Based Learning, or PBL – but it presupposes that Project Based Learning is the right idea for the problem in hand. Our challenge on hearing this How Might We statement is that, actually, the problem PBL is meant to be solving isn't clear.

The design team in question may not wish to share beyond their number what they eventually came up with through a process of team critique, but their final How Might We statement certainly makes clear what the problem is: 'How might we prepare teaching staff to move from general, dull and boring learning to delightful learning full of engagement and clarity?' It's wordy, but at least we know what the problem is, and what the vision will be.

3. Your language makes sense to a policy administrator – but if I were a kid I wouldn't know what you were talking about. Jargon is the bane of innovation. 'Anytime, anywhere student-focussed mobile learning' means too many things to too many people, and means nothing to another slew of folk who don't master eduspeak. 'Flexible spaces' is now such a loaded slogan that it equates almost instantly to beanbags and tables with wheels on the bottom.

The Twitter moniker @managerspeak will give you hours of entertaining education in how not to form an engaging problem statement that hooks your team into solving it: 'We need to foster a mindset that addresses heart-of-the-business non-linear thought leadership if we're to gain the competitive advantage.' Quite.

Aim for language a ten-year-old might understand and you'll have a more actionable problem to solve. At The American School in Japan, one group thought about parental expectations of the (high performing) school, and how that equated to their expectations of the kind of learning that might go on there, before creating this problem statement to explore: 'How might we find out what parents' expectations actually are of their first five days of school so that we can make the first ever days of school the best ones they ever have?'

No jargon, to-the-point, emotive and reflecting the empathy study this team had undertaken.

NEXT STEPS IN DEFINING THE CHALLENGE

- ✓ Make sure that all the design team bring all their ideas into physical form, and together into one place.
- ✓ What is your gut telling you from an initial look through what has been observed? Do you need to go back to fill in gaps? Are you missing detail or whole chunks of information? Now's the chance to go back to the immersive observation and get that done.
- ✓ Connect observations in as many ways as possible. Play about with combinations, opposites, contradictions. Don't settle for a 'good' clustering of observations first time around – seek the odd, the tension, the things that don't complement each other.
- ✓ Define the problem strictly with the phrase 'How might we...' Define multiple problems if you need to; don't try to make one problem statement solve multiple issues.
- ✓ Keep language concrete, in 'plain English'. Test your problem statement with your community – do they get it, do they feel it's important, does their body language tell you this when you share the problem statement with them?

THE THIRD HORIZON – REACHING FOR THE STARS

'Unless you dream, you're not going to achieve anything.'
Richard Branson

Ewan McIntosh

WHAT'S YOUR BHAG?

We have defined a distinct problem, sourced from a 'pain' of the people in our community. Now we have to frame a solution, and work out the road towards that solution. This is the point of any strategy.

Pick a small, persistent pain – constant littering around a school – and you can generate lots of small ideas, one of which will solve the problem.

Pick a bigger pain, and it might take more effort to get to a solution. These are the kinds of challenging problem that make the basis of a rich strategy, a rich Third Horizon.

Dreaming big is something that many perceive as futile – we can dream big, but it ain't going to necessarily happen. There is some truth in this.

But the notion of having a Big Hairy Audacious Goal, or a BHAG, is something that keeps coming back in the creative industries. A BHAG is an essential piece of vision that springs from having decoded a problem that needs solving, and is found in those companies which are decades or centuries old as well as those startups that are still fledglings.

Here are some famous BHAGs based on particularly wicked problems. Some are about making the world a better place, or changing the face of the Earth:

Amazon: Every book, ever printed, in any language, all available in less than 60 seconds.
Ford: Democratize the automobile.
Google: Organize the world's information and make it

universally accessible and useful.
JFK's Moon Challenge: This nation should commit itself to achieving the goal, before this decade is out, of landing a man on the moon and returning him safely to the earth.
Microsoft: A computer on every desk and in every home.
Motorola: Sell 100,000 TVs at $179.95.
SolarAid: To eradicate the kerosene lamp from Africa by 2020.
Nokia Siemens Networks: Connect 5 billion people by 2015.

Other BHAGs are more about beating the competition or leading the field:
Disney: Be the best company in the world for all fields of family entertainment.
Hewlett-Packard: Be one of the best managed corporations in the world.
Philip Morris: Become the front-runner in the tobacco industry.
   Others are about bettering themselves, or daring themselves to do more:

Sony: Embody changing the image of Japanese products as being of poor quality; create a pocket transistor radio.
IBM: Commit to a $5 billion gamble on System/360.

We might prefer some of these goals to others, we might see some of them, from our own bias, as more important than others. Whatever our view, these examples show us some interesting lessons for creating our own visionary ideas:

1. All these goals feel worthwhile for the organisations behind them.
2. The language is concrete and provides a direction that helps any employee or co-creator of a service or product to understand where it is headed.

3. None of them imply a world in need of improvement (other than the Sony one), something Benjamin Zander, the musician, conductor and visionary impresses upon us in the creation of any vision.

4. All the visions revolve around people and changing perceptions, habits or decisions.

5. But with these four points to bear in mind, how do we go from our defined problem of the First Horizon towards a visionary goal in our Third Horizon?

BIG IDEAS IN THE SMALL STUFF

Big ideas don't always spring from what we have identified in the First Horizon as the chief problem. We may have ended up with something really important, but relatively minor.

For example, constant littering in a school is a problem worth solving, but it feels 'silly' to a school leader to make that the school strategy. They'd be right – it's good, but it's not a BHAG.

We need to be able to solve those non-BHAG problems as they appear, maybe by teaching some of these Three Horizons or design thinking techniques to our teams and delegating challenging areas to them. That said, school leaders really need to sweat the small stuff if they are ever to spot the greatest opportunities for those BHAG moments.

During our immersion into the First Horizon, we talked about Richard Branson, the British entrepreneur with a knack for finding great problems to solve. A key trait of Branson is his constant note-taking. Most of the everyday challenges that he spots on his travels are ones that could have been sorted out already – we're not talking about building new aircraft (or building a new school), firing staff, or introducing hefty new policies on which all staff will have to be trained.

The small challenges that mean a lot for Branson have included the story of a passenger who lost his coat. The passenger had been relaxing with some pre-flight drinks in Virgin's renowned Upper Class lounge, and was perhaps so relaxed that, only as he sat down in the aeroplane, did

How To Come Up With Great Ideas and Actually Make Them Happen

he realise that he had left his rather expensive leather jacket back in the lounge. The aircrew apologised, but with the aircraft doors closed and the flight pushing back, it was too late to recover it now. Unbeknown to the passenger, aircrew contacted ground staff to see what could be done. Now, this was in the days of the legendary Concorde, the flagship of 'David' Virgin's arch-competitor, 'Goliath' British Airways.

Spotting an opportunity to solve this small problem and make a big impact, Virgin ground staff ran the jacket to the Concorde flight, which was due to leave shortly after the Virgin flight had already headed off.

Pulling a favour from BA staff, the ground crew got the jacket on board and picked up by a Virgin rep in New York when the Concorde flight landed. With the Concorde flight several hours shorter than the regular Virgin jet, the jacket was ready and waiting for the Upper Class passenger when he deplaned seven hours later.

Most upper class passengers are frequent flyers, with much opportunity to compare small things such as attention to detail, and make their airline choice accordingly. But frequent flyers can also be a pain.

Branson's financial officer reported that this regular, high-spending clientele kept stealing the beautiful, but expensive, salt and pepper cellars from their meal trays. How could they solve this problem, without taking away from the silver service?

Now, they are all marked on their base with the words: 'Stolen from Virgin Atlantic'; it doesn't stop them getting stolen, but it does make more of their friends consider flying with a fun airline.

These small changes, for a Head Teacher in a school, might seem like small details when there are so many other Important and Urgent things on their plates, but they are small details that directly influence how every person feels about their experience.

If Branson can get worried about salt cellars while he

buys up aircraft, sells off record companies and launches new companies the next day, what's the smallest detail each day that a Head Teacher or other senior leader can spot needing work?

It's in spotting these small details, in fact, that anyone in a school can become an innovation leader, as it's the solutions to these small problems that people notice, borrow and, yes, quite often steal.

It is no mistake that school staff, no matter the country, often correlate a 'good head of school' with one whom they see permanently, apparently, in the corridors of the school. Indeed, it is rare to find compliments from the staff for a Head whom they never see, holed up in the Leadership Suite – a physical space that, by its very nature, precludes innovation elsewhere.

Sweat the small stuff, boss. It makes a difference. And if you're not a boss yet, then sweating the small stuff, if Branson's story is anything to go by, will make you the boss soon.

CROSSING THE CHASM

Often, when we're coming up with ideas to solve a problem, we consider how we might come up with plenty of ideas. But has your team ever considered how many problems might actually be rolled up in what you've initially spotted?

In technology startups, it's not uncommon to have already begun developing the code, developing the idea itself, before you begin to really home in on what the real problem needing to be solved is. The startup then has to 'pivot', to move subtly (and sometimes lock, stock and barrel) to cater for that new emerging need.

It's not uncommon, either, for a startup to build a full working product or service that really works for a group of the population – normally for fellow programmers and startup 'geeks' – but which plateaus at the point where one might expect it to hit the mainstream.

This falling short of the big success you had hoped for in your idea is described by Geoffrey Moore in his book and theory of *Crossing The Chasm*. As Innovators and super Early Adopters seize a new idea, there is a significant gap to cross, a chasm, if the rest of your early adopters and the mainstream will adopt your idea.

Often, to cross the chasm, ideas have to be picked apart, carried over in parts, and reassembled, often in a different way, on the other side.

In short, you might not only end up with a different product, but you might have even found yourself a new problem needing solved as a result.

It's a complex journey, and many a startup has fallen

into the chasm, never to be seen again.

Do schools have this chasm to cross with their innovations and new ideas? Every time. In some environments, the School Leadership Team are that initial audience of Early Adopters, in other cases it might be the 'IT Working Group', or the 'Design Team'. Perhaps the IT Director and Business Managers see huge potential in their latest idea, but everyone else in faculty just fails to get it. And often that's as sophisticated as discussion around innovation gets: 'those people' either 'get it' or they 'don't get it', they are either 'innovative' or 'laggards'. There's no middle ground, even though the majority of folk inhabit that middle ground. It's no wonder that national technology 'innovations' that hold this attitude have failed so often – they've been ignoring the largest group of potential adulating fans!

In 2014, a dozen schools from the Richland 2 district in South Carolina participated in an innovation incubator, where their nascent ideas were put through the mill in bootcamps and online coaching.

A key challenge was that they all thought that they had defined 'The Idea' that would work. In many cases, the idea was indeed promising, and just needed perfecting. But a key learning in these ideas' early days was that there was no such thing as "The Idea", but "The Ideas", plural, that would appeal to different elements of their target audience.

For example, teachers Jeanne Blackburn, Alice Wofford and Sheri Barfield developed CrowdED, an online platform for local schools only which helped teachers reach out to local people to ask for donations of cash, time, expertise and resources for school projects.

Their initial idea was an obvious hook for educators who were already struggling to get visibility on wider, more global sites offering a similar service, such as DonorsChoose. But the initial idea didn't have any answers as to how to engage resisters, educators who didn't want to have 'outsiders' donating resources to their school, or thought the school should be self-sufficient in its resourcing.

Seeing this chasm led the team to expend much more effort on a new way of communicating what the service was for, and what was in it for these people: namely, this involved considering a bunch of offline activities to lure them in.

Another group in the incubator creates cookery videos between children and catering staff at the school, to encourage healthy eating. The initial group of students watching these videos are those who already like cooking – and eating – but on the other side of the chasm lies a large group of parents, students and even educators for whom it's a big ask to go onto a website to view cookery videos, and then go and cook some healthy food.

Realising this chasm existed, a second strand of activity was created to cater to their needs, whereby local supermarkets would eventually place recipe cards with the cookery show's URL next to the foodstuffs required for the recipes.

This way, the connection between healthy eating and the real target audience – people buying ingredients – is much more tangible, much easier to make, than hoping, fingers crossed, that the target audience will happen across the website and videos.

Every group has a chasm to cross, and they need thinking and discussion tools to cross it successfully with staff. These are the tools we're discussing throughout this section on the Third Horizon.

DEFINING YOUR BEACHHEAD STRATEGY

When you resign yourself to the fact that you'll never develop one idea for one homogeneous 'audience' again, you're left with a sobering question: 'Exactly who am I building my idea for?'.

It's sobering because it should feel like a big question. One concept to help break this down is the notion of working out your beachhead. It's a military metaphor.

The qualities of a beachhead for a soldier are daunting – the first prominent position of the beachhead is normally highly visible, open to attack from all sides and hard to defend as your team wrestle their way up the cliffs behind you. Once on top of the beachhead, you still have to fight tooth and nail to capture a few square feet, to let the rest of the platoon get up there with you. Once you've seized the beachhead, you probably then only have enough in the platoon to leave a few behind to hold the position and cover the rest of you as you head either left or right to take the rest of the coast, as you 'spread out'.

In startups, this feels the same. Amazon, when it launched, had to climb and attack the enormous beachhead of finding and buying books (the 'application') for people who craved more choice in their book-buying (the 'customer segment'). Once they had seized control of that market, they concentrated on offering that clientele more choice in their books, with their 'if you like this then you might like this' suggestions – the customer segment remained the same, but the application had changed.

Again they innovated – having seized this second application, it was time to introduce a third to this book-choice-loving segment: gift-giving.

At some point, having really taken over the attention of the book-choice-loving customer segment, Amazon felt it had a strong enough foothold to move down the other side of the coast in its beachhead: music. It began by offering those who loved choice in music the same large offering of CDs and DVDs that it had offered lovers of book choice with its paperbacks.

Once it had consolidated the notion of music choice, it kept hold of the same customer segment – music-choice-lovers – and put in a different application to them: music downloads.

It's therefore quite logical, viewed in this manner, that Amazon should merge those two concepts: downloads and books. Their third market application and third customer segment were those looking for choice in home electronics. The Kindle was but a step away down the beachhead, the logical next step as they further consolidated their position.

This same beachhead model is extremely useful for school innovators thinking about their next 'big idea', as its forces you somewhat to reduce this idea to one group of people at a time.

It helps deal with large numbers of people over time, but to cater, initially at least, for innovators in each customer segment. Who would be the various segments of people within a learning community for whom you are solving any given problem? It is not always the students first and foremost who stand to benefit most from an innovation, and it's invariably not the students who need to be won over first if an idea is to gain traction in the widest, deepest sense.

So if our first beachhead segment is to win over a group of teachers, then the first segment might be 'innovative teachers', with the subsequent adjacent segments being 'teachers in the Middle School', 'new teachers', or 'teachers who've expressed an interest in helping out'.

If students are the group to whom we are going directly with our innovation, then the first segment might be 'Grade 1 students', with adjacent segments being 'Grades 2-3', 'Grades 4-6', 'Middle School students', 'students at the transition to high school', and so on.

When we talk about parents, how far can we segment that far-from-homogeneous group? Mums, dads, carers, young mums, parents with multiple kids at our school...

The discipline in this process is not to believe that we can lump several segments together to be tackled at once. Different segments have different expectations and require different approaches, different versions of the same idea to appeal to them.

CHOOSE WHO YOUR IDEA IS FOR

The first step in developing a great idea to solve a problem is not, funnily enough, to come up with ideas. It is, according to hi tech audio firm LINN products, 'to choose your customer'.

CEO Gilad Tiefenbrun knows this well. His father's firm developed the world's best record turntable in the 1970s, and today under his helm provides the world's highest quality streaming music and music systems, with home music systems costing upwards of $20,000, often around the $50,000 mark.

When you make such a luxury product, for people prepared to pay for the difference in quality, you need to find those people first and discover what they really want and need, and whether the problem you're trying to solve exists for them. In LINN's case, solving this need for a specific person has become their vision, their BHAG:

Our network music players are the best way to listen to music, movies and games at home.

The BHAG makes perfectly clear what the mission of the company is: networked music which, from LINN at least, will be the best sound (not just 'really good') from any medium that you will ever hear, while at home (not in the office, or venue). Ambitious, yet useful in everyday decision-making by people in the firm, and for customers wondering whether they want just good, excellent or the best.

While the problems for education leaders are rarely finding clientele prepared to part with $50,000 for a music system, they are asking, in trying to solve any problem worth solving, an equivalent investment in time, energy, motivation, participation and goodwill. Just because you come up with a Big Hairy Audacious Goal does not mean that people will take to it, see the point in it, or want to

How To Come Up With Great Ideas and Actually Make Them Happen

participate in making it happen. Indeed, if you don't start with your 'customer' of the vision in mind, you're likely to have to start all over again further down the line.

Most politicians, leaders, teachers and parents would not hesitate to say that students, above all, are the chief 'customer' for any innovation that happens in learning.

This is a beautiful thought, a charming soundbite, a noble belief. In practice, most innovation in education requires multiple people, or actors, to get behind an idea and undertake their own part in achieving it. Therefore, having a vision that appeals most, or solely, to learners will not reach out in the same way as it would to, say, educators.

Have you ever heard educators complain that 'the big ideas' they generate never seem to come to anything? One chief reason for this is, perhaps, that while the intent is to improve the lives of students, the process to actually bring that improvement requires the vision to reach out in equal measure to those who might make it happen: parents, teachers, leadership, politicos, local business, and the students themselves.

At the end of the day: how many school vision documents set out what students can do for themselves to make their vision happen? Most of the time such documents put pressure on leadership and teachers – the people paid to be at school – to make the changes.

So how does one create a Third Horizon Big Hairy Audacious Goal that will appeal to all these constituents?

To go back to the practice of Gilad Tiefenbrun and his colleagues at LINN, and to look towards the decades of practice and research digested by MIT Entrepreneurship Center Director Bill Aulet, the answer lies in choosing your customer, user or target, one at a time:

Whose problem is it we're solving first and foremost?

Can we prioritise who we reach out to first, second, third?

Can we work out what kind of iteration of our idea will work at each stage of the journey, for each person to whom we're trying to reach out?

We are going to create ideas for the real needs of these people first and foremost, rather than us simply having an idea that we push onto them. *Pull* describes in great depth the difference between ideas borne of people's 'pain points', and ideas that are pushed upon them – the latter are those 'solutions looking for a problem' that people find it hard to get excited about.

In the formal education sector, this is a tricky mindset to achieve. Often, with many great exceptions, there is a resistance to changing anything in schooling towards what the kids or parents would like it to be – somehow we, the 'push-meisters', know better and others will have to change their behaviour to suit.

The 'customer-focussed' questions are vital to bear in mind, but we'll come to them in detail later. It is the principle that flavours our thinking for the process of coming up with an audacious idea: we need to have in the front of our minds the people for whom solving this particular problem will make the biggest difference.

For the moment, the 'Point of View' expressed in our 'How Might We…' problem statement will suffice as a marker for whom we are trying to solve this problem. Before we add too many constraints to the mix, it's more important to just come up with some ideas.

BEYOND PILOTS

Having this attitude towards all ideas being treated as equally important until they get to implementation (the Second Horizon) helps leaders get lots of action going on in a school, action that has been thought through and is based on genuine need, rather than on the latest fad.

It also helps in one other important regard: you will never have need of a pilot programme ever again. Most ideas about to be born in the Third Horizon start very small; teams developing them 'hold their ideas lightly'.

The audaciousness comes after an idea has been bounced around a fair bit, and all ideas are based, after all, on the sincere depth of understanding gained in an immersive First Horizon research phase and an approach to synthesis that has cornered a genuine problem worth solving.

Pilot programmes do the opposite: they lead to people creating working practices on the hoof (and not really being sure of their impact) instead of as part of a planned, reliable process. Outcomes of pilots are rarely of the BHAG variety – they are specifically designed to be small not big, safe not audacious, svelte not hairy, and their goals are lacking in ambition of scale. It's no surprise that most pilots in education seem to fail when asked to 'scale' to a wider group of participation.

In East Lothian Council almost a decade ago, the then Director of Education, Don Ledingham, had a vocal 'no-pilot' stance: just do it, was the policy.

Social media policy in 2005 was one area of my own work in this school district which, at the time, was hitting the headlines. Indeed, most schools today continue to have an inadequate policy for the use of social media for learning, including the publishing of students' images and names across social websites.

Social media use today is perhaps not considered 'innovative' in teaching and learning, but as a French and German teacher in Musselburgh, in 2004/5 we were creating Europe's first ever podcasts from a high school in a policy vacuum. It was probably better for it: fewer questions and fewer controls meant we were able to move faster than anyone else.

By 2006, though, across the East Lothian local authority, or district, social media use amongst teachers had grown from around a dozen blogging teachers to several thousand connected sites.

By this time, I was working on behalf of the Scottish Government, using East Lothian as a sandpit for innovative technologies use in learning. The need for a scalable policy was paramount. Keeping the reason for all this social media use in mind – to share knowledge, expertise and 'harness the crowd' – we developed a loose outline for a policy document covering the use of social media and mobile phone technology in and out of the classroom, for learning purposes.

It represented, in all truth, our initial ideation or brainstorm of what might be worth considering. It was our Third Horizon – small, and far off in the distance.

This outline was then shared on a wiki: anyone could edit the document and contribute to its evolution as their classroom practice evolved. Each year, the document was consulted once more to see if any seismic changes in technology or practice were reflected in new wording, and this wording would be adopted district-wide as policy.

The policy document and its accompanying permission forms for students are still available online, under a Creative Commons licence, for people to reuse in their own districts and schools. They provide a blanket common strategy for dealing in a flexible manner with an ever-changing field.

The pilot, the 'beta version', of our idea is, in fact, an ever-changing final idea. There is no such thing as a pilot.

IDEATION: GENERATING IDEAS

THE MINDSET TO CREATE

There are small forests of books available in your local airport or online bookstore that are designed to feed you tactics for coming up with ideas. Some suggest long walks, others recommend meditation, others still play with versions of brainstorming.

In my team's work, we've spent time with fashion designers, United Nations team leaders, telco call centre workers, as well as tens of thousands of teachers, helping them come up with ideas to solve some of the problems they identify from their initial research, observation and empathy studies.

Depending on the time you have, you can invent ingenious ideas in anything from four minutes to four months, but it needn't take long if you have some method for the controlled madness of ideation. You can transform meetings at the end of the day – those normally drab and tired affairs when everyone wants to get home – into brief encounters with creative genius and light-touch wonder.

A peculiar feature of the best genuine innovations is that they come in response to a 'user pain', the problem that really annoys people, gets up their nose, but which, for some reason, hasn't been resolved yet. Often, the idea to solve a problem might come along at the same time as the problem itself is seen. These are the one-in-a-million aha! moments that Nicholas Taleb describes as 'Black Swans'.

How To Come Up With Great Ideas and Actually Make Them Happen

We've talked much already about how to capture both of these – the steady immersion to identify 'pain' points of a problem, or the bugs list and ideas wallet to capture moments of frustration-turned-inspiration.

YES, AND... NO BUTS

All ideation processes, whether against the clock or not, require moments of non-judgement and judgement. Knowing which comes where, and ensuring that judgement takes place at some point, is vital.

In schools this is particularly important – it's where great practitioners put their formative assessment skills, and those of their students, to work. Initially, though, ideas need protecting.

In an exercise such as 100 Ideas Now, there is simply no time for people to get precious about their ideas, or to critique others'. So, as a facilitator in such an exercise, it's vital to make clear these rules of the game.

You don't need to be in ideating mode, though, to create a healthy environment for innovative thinking about a problem. In a staff meeting, why not enforce the 'Yes, and... no buts' rule? By forcing people (normally in a manner that involves a wry grin and chuckle) to change their normal 'Yes, but...' into a 'Yes, and...' you can help make ideas better.

Your harshest critics in the team can actually become your more creative team members, as these two small words help build on each other's ideas.

100 IDEAS NOW

There are five of you in a team, and you've just brought your problem observations together, and spotted the underlying issue that needs solving. So, if, as your facilitator, I gave you just 10 minutes to come up with 100 ideas together, how would you do?

This high-paced effort is one of the most popular activities and take-aways from our workshops, an idea we found in the must-have ideator toolkit *Gamestorming*. As a facilitator of it, though, you have some responsibility to keep in mind steps, or rules of thumb, that make this more than simply fast brainstorming.

First, this is an exercise that benefits from standing up. My team read somewhere that standing up helps with creativity, and gave it a go. The results spoke for themselves. We took almost identical groups of young, long-term unemployed people in a creativity and employment programme we created for a fashion brand.

Those who had been sitting down could produce about 60-90 ideas in ten minutes. Those who had been standing for the duration, and followed the other simple rules, below, produced up to 160 ideas in the same time.

Second, the process benefits from individuals working alone, in silence, for at least a couple of the ten minutes.

Individual brainstorming initially prevents the team quickly descending into group-think, getting stuck in a rut of the initial ideas that the (loudest) first contributors have provided.

Third, every idea gets written down, either by one scribe for the team or by everyone in the team, as they come up with their idea. Having an independent scribe is useful, as all the ideas get written down. Having a scribe who doesn't know it's their job might mean some ideas get 'policed' early, and don't appear in the final list.

Fourth, the facilitator should keep time, and call it out with increasing passion as the clock approaches zero. Good facilitation increases the pace, and the more ideas are committed, the more chance you get a good one or two at the end. I tend to use an app on my phone.

Fifth, at about six minutes in, people start to seriously dry up, with even the most juicy problems to solve. This is normally the point that all the 'serious' and 'sensible' ideas have been provided, so a change of tack is required.

BEST AND WORST

If I said that your worst solutions for the challenges you're facing might just be your best way out of a tight spot, would you believe me?

As we stated earlier, 'Yes, and...' is a crucial ingredient for Ideation and working within the Third Horizon in general. For this next technique, which is from my friend and Stanford creativity guru Professor Tina Seelig, 'Yes, and...' is vital, even when you feel a little silly saying it.

In every organisation, but particularly in schools, people want to come up with great ideas; we want to do our 'best'. When you ask a room of teachers (or any professional for that matter) to come up with their 'best' solutions to a problem you often tend to get great ideas, but not always the best ones.

They can be contrived and almost always involve some self-censorship from the team: people don't offer anything up unless they feel, explicitly or subconsciously, that it will get buy-in from the rest of the team or committee.

Back in 2010, at a time when education budgets had never been smaller and were only going to get even smaller still, the thinking of leadership and staff could default to the 'old ways' of doing things – expensive committees, organisations, meetings, 'experts'. In straitened times, this way of working and thinking just won't cut it any more. It adds more time and expense to the process of solving the problem, reducing the number of people who can actively participate in solving it, and often leads to the 'same old, same old', the very kind of idea that generated the problem in the first place.

In a workshop back in 2010, therefore, I was keen to offer a different process to the leadership teams from police, fire, health and education services in the Scottish Borders region. How?

I asked people for their 'worst' solutions to the budgetary challenge they were facing. Ask people to come up with the most daft ideas they can to solve any given problem and they tend not to hold back at all – laughs are had and the terrible ideas flow.

And while the initial suggestions might feel stupid, pointless or ridiculous to the originating team members, these awful ideas can take on a spectacular new lease of life in the hands of another, unrelated group.

By insisting on a 'Yes, and...', rather than a 'Yes, but...' approach, a fresh set of eyes can turn these 'worst' ideas into the ones that will save money, improve service, or make people happier in the workplace.

These Scottish Borders officials came up with some genius 'bad' ideas, turned good through the process:

- Reduce cleaning costs by scrapping school cleaners. Yes, and... instead, we'll get the students to clean the 2 square metres around the area in which they are standing at 2pm every day.
- Reduce the costs of maintaining school grounds by no longer using Council environmental services to mow the grass. Yes, and... we'll get students to swap the neat lawns for some self-grown fruit and vegetables, leading to cheaper, better and fresher produce in school meals while also teaching youngsters about crop cycles and basic biology. We could even generate some extra money by selling extra produce to the community, or generate good will by giving it away to those families who occasionally struggle with the bills.
- Reduce the money spent on transporting children to school by stopping taxi runs from remote areas. Yes, and... we'll seek out parents to get some regular carsharing started. And we can make a feature of the diverse locations our students live in to create a massive start-of-term expedition to explore the area on foot, and see how close and how far students live from school.
- Improve the quality of service provision by forming a committee made up of everyone in the community.

Yes, and... you can call in to local radio and share who you think has made the biggest improvement in your local services (the refuse collector who always replaces the lid on your bin and cleans up rubbish, for example), but the result is given anonymously. That way, everyone in the Council thinks it might be them and adjusts their behaviour accordingly.

HOW ONE 'STUPID' IDEA COULD SAVE £12.5M A YEAR

I don't know the precise figure spent on fruit and vegetables, cleaning and gardening throughout schools in the UK, but these ideas, applied nationally, could have a positive effect on what and how students learn, as well as saving at least a few million (window cleaning alone is £25,000 a year in one English borough, which nationally would lead to a saving of at least £12.5m a year).

THE MINDSET TO HONE DOWN

NEW, USEFUL, FEASIBLE
My colleague Tom Barrett was working with me to show some of these ideation techniques to a new group of secondary school teachers with whom we were working in Sydney.

We sat on our balcony one evening, aware that there was already some scepticism in the room about the creative approach of design thinking on the one hand, and its place in a new curriculum which was perceived as stringent on the other. We sought out something that would add a more analytical element to ideation, and underline that, in fact, the design thinking process is a ying-yang, analytical/creative approach. After all, most techniques are based on gut instinct and discussion. Was there a technique that would help maybe unearth different ideas from what our guts were saying during one of these ideation sessions?

The result was New, Useful, Feasible. First, you need some way to narrow down your ideas from 100+ to something more manageable – your top eight, dozen or half dozen.

We often use 'stick-a-vote', where each team member can use their gut to choose their top five 'sensible' ideas, and then we give them an additional three stickers to mark out the 'silly' ones that might have the kernel of genius. We then plot them vertically down the lefthand side of a table, with the headings New, Useful and Feasible on top.

The work of the team is then to score each idea in each category, out of ten:

- How new is the idea for our school, or in the world?
- How useful is the idea for solving the problem we identified?
- How feasible is it for us to pull this idea off?

Once all the scores have been tallied, there is normally at least one clear winner, and some interesting second and third place ideas that might not have been considered before.

At this point, teams might take the ideas as they are, or begin playing with them: combining ideas to see what emerges or flipping them around to the opposing statement to see if there's something interesting in there.

By this point, though, based on the ease with which they are coming up with both quantity and quality of ideas, teams are also acutely aware of whether they have hit on a rich problem worth solving or whether, in fact, the problem is weak in the first place. This can be the point, sometimes, where it's time to go back to the observations and research notes to see whether the problem was right in the first place.

And, even if teams are convinced they have The Idea, it's time to start communicating that idea to others, and almost certainly time to change it once more. If the team has already generated hundreds of ideas through this process, then it's now far less painful to have them altered, built upon or even killed by others. There can always be another hundred new ideas tomorrow.

WORK OUT WHAT YOU'RE NOT

If you are spoiled for choice in the ideas generated, and can't choose one based on the gut instinct of the team or a New, Useful, Feasible type approach, then it's worth looking at what you're not trying to be or achieve.

Often, if lots of other options already exist to solve a problem, then we call this a Red Ocean – innovators avoid Red Oceans, and seek out innovation elsewhere. The Red Oceans are those seas filled with sharks fighting over the same small fish – the red is the blood from the wounds they inflict upon each other.

Blue Oceans are the clear blue oceans that the founders

in any startup company will seek. To find your innovative idea in a Blue Ocean, where no one comes close to beating you down, you need to seriously analyse what else is out there in the competition, and see whether your idea might just become better from being changed, changed away from the way the competition does things.

The cupcake industry is a Red Ocean. Every town is spoiled for choice in providers of cupcakes. A cupcake factory shop where you can design your own and have it made is not: it's a fresh idea no one is doing (as far as I know) that sits in a lush expanse of Blue Ocean.

Yakatori restaurants in Tokyo would mark Red Ocean territory – there are great places selling this skewered chicken in most districts already. Yakatori in Edinburgh, Scotland, would be somewhat more of a Blue Ocean. Take the same concept, though, and change the category to 'restaurants', and there Edinburgh is now just as crowded a Red Ocean market. Knowing what you are, and what you are not, and communicating that effectively is part of forming the big vision of the Third Horizon.

The textbook example of this was shared with me during an MIT Entrepreneurship Center workshop series at the University of Edinburgh. It came towards the end of two extensive, intensive days exploring our own companies and, as everyone's mind began to turn to the post-workshop proceedings, it was rather Ã propos that the final case study should be about wine.

Yellow Tail is a wine that, over a decade ago, was little known outside its domestic market, in Australia. In 2001, Australia's Casella Winery introduced Yellow Tail into the highly competitive American market. This small and unknown vineyard had expected to sell 25,000 cases in their first year – they ended up selling nine times that. By the end of 2005, the firm had sold over 25 million cases and later could claim to be the bestselling bottle of red wine in the world, outstripping Californian, Italian and, yes, even French brands.

Key to this success was mapping out what Yellow Tail was not, and what it aspired to be. This exercise was not undertaken in a windowless boardroom. They got out to see what was going on, and where they could take things. They modelled Genchi Genbutsu.

Their research showed that people in the early 2000s in the US had a choice between expensive 'good wine' and cheap 'not-so-good' wine. They discovered that America was, above all, mostly a nation of beer drinkers (wine drinkers were the minority). They found out that many of those not drinking wine were put off by the jargon, the pompous labelling and descriptions of 'noses' and 'heritages'. They just wanted to buy a good bottle of wine, not too expensive, and not something that would embarrass them if they brought it to a house party.

Two tools are useful in defining what a new idea – in this case, a new wine on the market – might have to do to mark itself out, and to know what it is not trying to be.

First of all, the factors of the existing attempts in the market are plotted on an x axis, and their importance to the consumer graded out of a notional '100 points'. So, with traditional wines in the early 2000s, they all placed importance on outlining the fine heritage of the wine, using wine buff jargon, showing illustrations of the vineyards and grapes, using certain austere fonts on the label, and so on.

In fact, the only real differentiator between a great wine and not-so-good wine, other than the taste, was often the price. Outlining these shows that there is room for differentiation on all fronts, and that cost of the wine could be left out as a priority.

Price points were not stopping people buying wine, after all. Something else was.

The second tool one might have used to harness this initial research is 'Reduce, Raise, Eliminate, Create'. The illustration shows how each of these marketing research factors could be plotted. First of all, we plot existing factors of which users are tired: jargon, the heritage on the wine labels, the overly complex grape varieties. We relegate these to 'Reduce' (if we feel that they are needed still) or 'Eliminate' (if we decide, based on our immersion in the First Horizon, that we don't need those factors any more).

Some factors might be worth making more of, as in the status quo they are not harnessed as much as they should be, and so we 'Raise' their importance. With more innovative space in which to operate, we are now free to 'Create', to ideate around some new concepts that might create difference in the current market and appeal to new users. This way, we carve out space for our new idea in people's busy lives.

This two-stage process is incredibly useful in an education environment, where much of the status quo feels immovable – it's just been around too long. It helps show that the baby needn't be thrown out with the bathwater. Imagine that a key problem we have unearthed is that curricular topics are deemed narrow and boring by students. Well, we can't throw out our curriculum. We can keep many elements, but reduce their importance: perhaps we place less emphasis on individual curricular targets in the International Baccalaureate, but raise the importance of other elements, such as the Strategic Targets in that curriculum that many schools push to the background of planning units of work.

We might eliminate the need for the narrow learning targets to be mapped out in some kind of 'logical sequence' – the kind of suitcase curriculum logic that happens in most schools when people have built curriculum as they've gone. We might create something new: a curricular mapping tool that helps teachers recognise retrospectively when students have actually attained those specific learning targets, and provides students with information about what learning targets they might want to address, having not achieved them within the run of a specific school project.

How To Come Up With Great Ideas and Actually Make Them Happen

In Dublin, Ireland, three Technology Institutes are being brought together into the city's newest university, the Technological University for Dublin. Once the administrative elements of such an ambitious project start to emerge, there is a natural nervousness on the part of lecturers, students and other employees about what such a change might mean. Each of the Institutes has developed its own culture and distinct appeal to local students.

In order to work out what a new institution might mean, we held a few intensive workshops over a day and a half. The first day was spent looking almost exclusively at the way things are, the status quo, and testing the entrenched assumptions of why things were the way they were in the first place. We also spent that first day exploring how other learning institutions organised their learning and teaching, their course structure and so on – provocations to begin setting the proverbial cat among the pigeons.

The result was fascinating. Having split over 100 students, lecturers and leadership into smaller groups of three to five members, I had thought that each table would create something quite unique – they all had different stimuli, different experience around the table and different provocations from me.

Yet, by the end of the day, it was clear that there was some consensus on which elements of the status quo this particular large group thought should be reduced in importance (lectures); which would be raised (interactive teaching, something the Institutes have pride in already); what would be eliminated (the assumption that all first-year students are 18; mature and international students offered an interesting new take on that initial Higher Education experience); and what they might create (university careers spanning eight, not four years, where working in industry was as important as the course, where mini-courses might inform younger first-year entrants where their passions, and therefore future study, might lie).

From analysing the status quo from the First Horizon, we can already begin to have some creative instinct as to what a fresh solution might look like.

IT'S IN IF...
Another safety net in the process of ideation, when you feel you're getting stuck or heading down the wrong path, is to look back to your First Horizon materials, the evidence of the problem at the heart of what you're trying to build a solution to. From this data and the initial ideas that have been produced, your team can begin to form a values-based list of what factors might mean an idea is 'in' and which factors would lead to an idea going 'out', being marked off the list. This is an 'It's In If...' list.

I first came across this notion from the photographs of a Project Manager friend and former colleague, Jamie Arnold. Arnold is Project Manager on the United Kingdom's biggest IT challenge of this decade: making hundreds of Government websites one, and making them easy to use on things that really matter to citizens.

The 'It's In If...' list that he and his team created outlines in clear terms what any team member needs to know when making a decision about whether to continue a Government web service from the First Horizon, adapt it for better use, or kill it.

It's in if...
- Only government can do it (can anyone else do it better?)
- Citizens want it (we can tell this through traffic, interaction and what people search for)
- It explains rights and obligations
- It's an actionable transaction that can be carried out digitally (that is, you don't have to go into an office to do it.
- The public's behaviour doesn't have to change in order to undertake the service.

This actionable list is much more useful for an ideation session, for coming up with an ambitious vision, strategy or solution to a problem, than the average mission statement. It's actionable, checkable, unambiguous. It empowers the maximum number of people in an organisation to make decisions on the innovation at hand, without having to ask permission or clarification of the leadership.

THERE IS ALWAYS COMPETITION

Working out what you're not, working out if an idea is 'in' with your mission or not, is the first step in taking a wide range of ideas and honing it down.

A key element of this thinking is that of competition. Every idea competes with others. In the world of technology startups, this is crystal clear: over the past six years I can't count how many 'it's-Google-meets-Facebook-meets-Pinterest's I've had to let down gently. In schools and the public sector in general, the notion of competition is less clear, and often one that makes public servants uneasy, with its notions of failed public-private partnerships or unreachable targets.

This is not what we mean when we ask you about your idea in terms of where it might compete. We simply want to find its point of differentiation, the reason people might care enough about your idea to use it, get involved with it, harness it.

One of the clearest, most algorithmic ways of thinking about competition was created by the hundreds of entrepreneur authors behind the tome Business Model Generation. It is a superb publication, and has become a regular dip-in bible for startups, not-for-profits and governments as they consider launching new ideas. It provides an exhaustive rundown of the different ways ideas can compete, the way they can stand out and become useful for people. In education, as in startups, you can help develop your idea by really defining how it's going to compete with every other initiative or policy document crossing your colleagues' desks.

Don't be put off by the age-old 'we just have too much on our plates as teachers, we can't cope with anything new'. If your idea is both great and its benefit clear to people, they do make room for it. Part of making the benefit clear is to outline the key competitive edge your idea has over similar, but not as good, ideas:

Newness

Just being new can be enough to set your idea crisp in people's minds. Obviously, it doesn't continue to work very long, so if newness is your key card to play, you need to bear in mind additional elements that are significant enough on their own to require a separate 'launch' later on, to bring attention for themselves in their own right.

For example, if you want to introduce a new one-to-one tablet programme, you have new on your side for a couple of months. But newness can be maintained by introducing people, in a planned, staged manner, to the all the new ways the devices can be used. The staged discovery of how it can be used as a presentation device, an information management tool, an art palette, a music studio...

At NoTosh, we developed the use of a tablet computer, the iPad, in a truly innovative way by turning it into a flexible multi-format notebook for formative assessment learning logs. Although the devices are now several years old, the means of using them appeared totally new to people, reinvigorating their use of an 'old' tool.

Performance

Sometimes, when I'm choosing medium-haul flights, I notice the large difference in flight time. On checking the aircraft type I realise why: the cheaper flight's equipment is a new, environmentally friendly, but low-powered, turboprop, while the more expensive jet is half an hour faster, and more detrimental to the environment.

Here, performance could be one or the other, depending on the mindset of the customer: environmentally, performance is high on the turboprop, which appeals to green-conscious travellers like me, while pure speed is the high performance factor of the jet my more rushed compatriots might take.

In schools, performance can seem like a dirty word, linked to target-setting and testing. But, much in the same way as the performance of aeroplanes can be seen in a different light, so, too, can 'performance' in the realm of education.

In our design thinking work with schools, for example, we're seeing reports from teachers that this way of thinking and planning learning is speeding up their coverage of swathes of content. The performance gain is something like two weeks to cover six weeks' worth of content if it had been taught in 'traditional' ways. This performance gain then frees up four more weeks to undertake ideation and prototyping activities that, normally, there is little time to do as well.

Customisation
I often wonder what the designers at a company like Apple make of people customising the design that they slogged so hard to perfect: stickers layered up on cleanly designed laptop lids, lurid pink or football-badge-emblazoned iPhone covers...

Many other products and ideas end up being customised when it was not their creators' intent: fan fiction writers 'customise' the novels they have read, creating new versions that are relevant, engaging reading for millions online. Then there are other products or ideas that it would be strange to customise at all: you would not paint a red Ferrari with yellow stars.

Teachers rarely take another teacher's resource and use

it 'out of the box'. They want to make it their own, they want to customise it. Innovators in education are often loath to let others take their ideas and make it their own. Some of this is maybe down to the fact that most educator innovators are innovating in their own, non-overtime weekends and evenings, and they want some form of credit or tip of the hat for their ideas.

Some of it comes down to developing ideas so extensively and deeply that they have become too difficult to unpick and customise.

But customisation, the potential for people to take your idea and make it their own – and often without credit – is an incredibly powerful vehicle for getting ideas to spread far and wide. Take TeachMeet, the unconference for teachers by teachers, which takes place around the world every week of the year. It's a free event where teachers can sign up to give a seven-minute talk or a two-minute nanopresentation to peers. No PowerPoint is allowed, no commercial companies are allowed to 'sell'. And that's it.

Thousands of teachers attend one of these events every month, hundreds claim it's the best professional development they've ever had. They might have attended a behemoth event, such as the annual ones in London or Sydney, or they might start one themselves in a local café with half a dozen other colleagues.

The idea began in 2006, when I wanted to meet up and chat with colleagues that I never got a chance to see, colleagues who were blogging, podcasting and using technology in fascinating ways. It quickly became the antidote to the 'official' conference in the city of Edinburgh at the time: no keynotes, no sponsors, no fixed schedule. Half a dozen of us, and one Will Richardson, who was indeed keynoting at the event up the road, huddled around pub tables at The Jolly Judge, with nothing but ourselves, some wifi and a pint to pass the evening away. It was, indeed, one of the best professional development experiences any of us had had.

Within six months, I had created a website and a name – TeachMeet – with some very simple 'rules' for running a good event, borrowed from my time organising Scotland's first BarCamp for tech entrepreneurs.

Almost immediately, the event started getting customised. David Muir, a former lecturer of mine at Strathclyde University, created TeachEat, after the event. The nano-presentations didn't exist in the beginning; they came at the point where more presentations than time came along, and more nervous first-timers wanted something less overbearing than 'presenting' to colleagues.

Basically, this unconference flourished when it moved from being a fixed thing run by a group of people to a flexible, organic, customisable format that anyone, anywhere, could make their own, while continuing to guard the core principles that make it distinct from other similar (but not anywhere near the same) offerings.

Getting The Job Done
I fly a lot for work. On nearly every aircraft I take, looking out to just under the wing, I always see the same crest: Rolls Royce. The British car manufacturer makes more money these days from its airline engines that transport millions of tourists and business people around the world every day.

In 2011, a Qantas jet with these engines had an engine problem, one that made the headlines, but thanks to a competitive element Rolls Royce have over everyone else, that aircraft would not stay on the ground longer than it absolutely had to. Rolls Royce's competitive element in the airline engine business is that they Get The Job Done.

If one of their engines develops a fault, it will be fixed or, at worst, replaced, in super quick time. For every hour on the ground, compensation to the airline will go towards the inconvenience. So confident are Rolls Royce in their engines that they guarantee that they will get the job done.

In education innovations, it's sometimes not entirely

clear what the job is. We're spoilt for choice, in fact, when it comes to resources, professional development, potential equipment or software we might purchase, and generally we're limited with funds.

Knowing what the problem is in the first place (aeroplane engines are hugely complex but mostly reliable; but they need expensive expert assistance when they do go wrong) helps come up with a solution that will Get The Job Done for everyone (we'll group every purchase into a global repair programme, meaning we employ fewer experts and fly them out to repair when necessary).

No teachers complained when mass-printing photocopiers were introduced to schools: the problem of the time, quality and limited numbers traditional machines could copy with the teacher turning the wheel were eliminated by a machine which, when you pressed the button, did whatever you asked it to. It even stapled the document for you. It got the job done.

Most schools in those early days were not too bothered about the brand, how customisable the settings were, or even the price (they were eye-wateringly expensive machines compared to the older model). It was all second place next to the fact it Got The Job Done, and freed teachers up to do their actual job: teaching.

What is the job that a virtual learning environment is there to get done? What is the job that a term of professional development efforts around formative assessment is there to get done? How often does 'Getting The Job Done' appear as an innovation in your school? Perhaps it's the one competitive category we could all work harder on.

Brand and Status
Apple had just launched the iPad, and the world went into a frenzy. The education world was no different. Within a few weeks of the product launch I read in online newspapers about the first school in a particular US state

who had created an 'innovative iPad Lab'.

From the story there was not a great deal of educational thought going into this purchase. There was, however, a love affair with the brand, something that had the school administration, school finance team and the journalists falling over themselves in a bid to recount the 'innovation' involved in the purchase. They were not alone. Many administrators talked less about the pedagogy behind their decisions, and more about the 'star power with kids' that the device had.

Cut to the Cedars School of Excellence in the West Coast of Scotland, a few days after this US school's iPad Lab has been created, and you have Fraser Spiers and his team creating a world-class installation of iPads, where every student has their own, teachers take part in collegiate sessions sharing ideas on using them, Fraser (a 'distinguished' Apple Distinguished Educator if ever I've seen one) leads the development of guides to act as aide memoires for teachers as they totally redevelop certain units of work in the transformative light of what this new machine can help them do.

One of these schools' competitive values in making the same investment in innovation was the Brand and Status offered by the iPad – getting the press release out in super-quick time, laying claim within days to having the world's first whole-school iPad deployment (well, in a Lab, available to the whole school) were the top priorities. The other school's plan was built on a different competitive element: perhaps it was newness although, in light of the accompanying effort to make sure the machines were used in educationally sound ways, it feels more like Performance was the key driver.

Using Brand and Status as a competitive element for driving your own idea is fine, if you already have Brand and Status. It takes time to build, and normally you build it through innovations that have one of these other competitive elements in prominence:

TKMaxx have built an amazing business on Cost Reduction (with quality produce), one that means their brand, over time, is a reason people are happy to tell their friends they're going;

Ferrari have built a business on Performance, something with which their brand has become so synonymous that many people sport Ferrari products other than the car (scarves, hats, seat covers for their Fiat);

Apple have built a business on Accessibility, as they made home computing a reality for many who were not convinced by the MS DOS green screens of the early 80s. They gave access to something that only a few had experienced, and continue to do so with every new product launch;

Burberry plc have built a brand that dominates the luxury fashion landscape, a brand built on Getting The Job Done and Risk Reduction (they provided the protective clothing for Shackleton's expedition across the South Pole, the Wright Brothers' transatlantic flight, Edmund Hillary's world-first climb up Everest and every First World War soldier's trench coat).

When you're developing your own innovative ideas for school, there's normally no brand of your own to rely upon. One might lean on the brand of others – in education technology this is a frequent ploy – but this might be nothing more than Newness, and so something more might be required alongside to make your idea stand up and compete with the rest.

Risk Reduction
MyPolice was one of my final investments at Channel 4. Its founders, two recent Glasgow School of Art graduates, had developed an online service that reduced a significant

risk for senior police officers, that they might receive a poor inspection report for their capacity to know whether or not they provided a good police service.

Such a notion – 'what is a 'good' police service?' – is incredibly difficult to make tangible but, through two large-scale trials, Lauren Currie and Sarah Drummond, barely in their 20s, cracked it through a community-driven site for whose raw data police forces were more than happy to pay handsomely. These entrepreneurs had found a user pain – an important but hard-to-quantify part of the police inspection routine – and solved it through a service designed to reduce the risk of bad or non-existent data in this domain.

Schools are already experts in risk reduction as a competitive value: internet filters, health and safety equipment, school trip risk assessments... Risk reduction is a powerful tool already in education, and makes plenty of dollars for the companies that peddle in a particularly negative version of it, but few of them create what can be called 'innovative' solutions in education. Most are copy-and-paste commodities with a large market ready to buy.

However, risk reduction, taken in the positive sense, can be highly innovative. What about innovative ideas that reduce the risk of schools killing the creativity in their students' lives? Or Learning Rounds which reduce the risk of teachers forgetting what it's like to learn as a teenager at High School?

What about rethinking teacher professional development altogether to reduce the risk that teachers are exposed to ideas which are a waste of their time (if we know what makes a difference to children's learning, then why do we spend time on unrelated initiatives, reports and training days?).

Cost Reduction
There are plenty of expensive products that reduce your costs over time. Every winter I get sent brochures trying to

make me part with significant sums of cash for solar panel installation at my home. Notwithstanding my scepticism of Scottish summers ever generating enough solar energy to power a family home, such products are, in fact, on the basis of appealing to my equally Scottish attitude towards saving money. With only Scottish summers to power them, my young daughters will have graduated from university before the panels pay for themselves, but in the lifetime of the building, and of those panels, the overall energy costs of the house will be reduced.

Innovations in education that reduce costs are incredibly hard to pull off. Generally, the innovations cost a lot of money upfront (like the solar panels), and schools' annualised budgets fail to provide the capital required. At our firm, we provide a retainer service which, over time, reduces the cost of professional development to well below that of our competitors.

The challenge for some smaller schools is that the commitment to a long-term relationship with one provider of professional development feels risky. Cost reduction in both cases is challenging for the customer to take advantage of because of (a) initial high costs or (b) the perception of making a decision that will affect the long term. School leadership, if it's not careful, can fall into a habit of thinking cheap and short term, resulting in longer-term expense.

As an innovator, it's vital to think around these challenges, and see whether your idea's key selling point for schools is reducing their costs. And can you reduce their costs without having to charge for a large upfront investment, or without people feeling they are locked into a relationship they've not yet had a chance to test out?

Price
Startups tend to thrive on price – the internet is, after all, where most people perceive the best price as being 'free', and the second best 'the cheapest'. It also lends the startup

some peculiar business challenges. If you're reducing costs for your users, how can you still make enough money to support your business?

Schools often look at their offering and don't think price comes into it, unless they are international or independent schools perhaps. But 'Price' doesn't always mean chasing the lowest price. There are plenty of reasons why charging a high price – or charging for a service when no one else does – is beneficial in trying to get people to take part in your idea or innovation. We are dubious, for example, if we see a Gucci handbag on sale for less than $400, unless we are in an outlet store, when we expect the price to be lower. Context is everything.

If you are a state school doing a great innovative project, it's a combination of plaudits and flattery that help other schools, in the early days, come around to visit gratis. There comes a point, though, where the way you're doing it is clearly not a commodity – people are travelling from the other side of the planet to observe your ways and means! At this point, finding a price that reflects prestige (high), the openness of your learning community (free) or the honesty of your offering (covering basic costs) tells people a lot about where you think your innovation stands. Low price for an innovation you're creating, or buying, is not always best.

For example, in Portugal, it was the purchase of an incredibly low-priced personal computer for a national one-to-one laptop programme that led to its ultimate failure – the device wasn't valued for anything other than a fast buck on eBay, and a similar low investment had been made into teacher development in the use of technology. Low price as a competitive value of the project ultimately led to it succeeding less well than it might have done.

Accessibility
Accessibility in education innovations often means providing a technological solution that every child can

access. Sometimes, historically, this has meant that innovations which are superb for the majority of children are shelved because they cannot be used by a minority. This has been useful in forcing producers to create content that is accessible, technologically, to everyone.

But this is not what we mean by accessibility in the world of startups.

If accessibility is your key competitive edge, it means that you offer access to a world that, previously, people could only have dreamed of. The airline Emirates opened up luxury to people who couldn't normally afford it, by offering Business Class fares one third the price of their competitors. Hulu, Apple and Netflix opened up access to beautiful BBC drama to the broadest of American audiences, not just those who flew to Europe every year and bought the boxed sets. Amazon opened up reading to the masses, encouraging more people to read books than have ever read books before (with the demise of the high street book store, which had its chance throughout the twentieth century, I feel quite happy giving Amazon most credit for the astronomical heights reading hits today).

In education, innovations that offer accessibility are surprisingly common. Khan Academy offers free access to maths tuition and coaching that, previously, was only available to rich kids. YouTube itself makes accessible some of the world's best natural history, science, artistic and musical content to the masses, where they'd have had to pay for it in the past (I remember purchasing educational drumming movies on VHS at $60 a pop as a teenager – the content is now available, legally too, for free on YouTube, Vimeo and the like).

Convenience
7-Elevens have their convenience baked into the brand: wherever you go in the world you know what time the shop opens and closes, at the very least. One also understands the pain of not having this convenience on

arriving Saturday evening in the countryside in Italy – you stand a chance of being rather hungry until Monday morning when the stores once more open.

Convenience has been a staple of startups. LoveYourLarder.com was a startup I helped out in its early days. Its competitive edge started out as one of price: it would make farmers' market type products available at the lowest price. But, in the end, this wasn't where the potential in the innovation lay.

LoveYourLarder's customers, the type of people who wanted to buy farmers' market produce, were not concerned with saving a pound here or there. They had money already to shop at farmers' markets, and busy jobs to pay for it. What they lacked was the time to visit every week. They might only manage once a month. With LoveYourLarder they could shop at any time they wanted to and get the same farmers' market produce. LoveYourLarder's competitive edge was not newness or luxury - maybe it could have aligned itself with convenience.

IDEATION: REFINING IDEAS SPECIFICITY VERSUS FLEXIBILITY

Having narrowed down a large number of ideas, played around with their feasibility and competitive stance, and combined this with other ideas to create something distinctive, there comes a point where expressing that idea to people outside the process is necessary. Doing this is easier said than done. Design guru Tim Brown points out that 'poor design briefs are not normally the ones with too many constraints..., but the ones that take all opportunity for discovery and surprise away. The design thinker has a stance that seeks the unknown, embraces the possibility of surprise, and is comfortable with wading into complexity not knowing what is on the other side.'

This embracing of the unknown is something that sits uneasily with many education leaders of innovation, particularly as they develop and hone down ideas for what their Third Horizon vision might be.

Yet, maintaining a degree of flexibility is vital. If we are too specific too early on in this Third Horizon phase, then we stand to create a dull, boring or failing idea for our vision. If we can maintain some specificity, have the people we are trying to serve in mind from our First Horizon immersion, then there is room also for continued flexibility as we tweak our good ideas to make them great.

BUILDING BETTER IDEAS THROUGH CREATIVE CONFLICT

Scotland-based educators and innovators Graham Leicester, Keir Bloomer, Denis Stewart and Jim Ewing released a short book, *Transformative Innovation in Education*, which had a powerful effect on school leadership across the country.

They applied the Three Horizons, a way of thinking about innovation one normally found in big business and management consultancies, to the specific context of curriculum change in Scotland. They reframed things in a way that could help any innovator in education to set up a constructive 'creative conflict'.

This kind of conflict is commonplace and indeed essential in the creative or innovation industries: we need to have a safe environment in which to play out all the potential ways our big, audacious idea might be shot down by others (the conflict) and explore how those potential conflicts will make our idea better (the creative part).

Many of the exercises we've suggested so far help our innovation team unveil either the conflict or the creative potential, but few bring both together in a structured way. In the creative industries, such as fashion and technology, this creative conflict often occurs in a haphazard way, and relies upon the guile and wit of the participants in the innovation team to work through the conflict and generate a solution to the challenge in hand. The trial and error shown in the various Virgin stories shared here are evidence of that. For educators working on specific innovation projects, it is far more useful to have a more predictable, less haphazard process to structure the discussion, and protect our nascent ideas from being shot down too early.

Key to the tool is bringing together the evidence from our First Horizon once more, and seeking what underlying values inform the status quo. These are referred to as Rock Values, implying that they are unlikely to move or change any time soon. Meanwhile, the creative hubbub we have experienced as part of the Third Horizon feels more like an exciting whirlpool, and so Whirlpool Values are sought from the wide range of ideas we have generated. Often, the values extracted from these two Horizons feel at odds with each other.

The first thing to realise, though, is that neither side is 'correct' or 'right' or 'innovative'. Most education around the world is set up for things to be considered as either Good or Bad, Correct or Wrong, but in innovation anything can be fatal if it's the only means through which innovation is created. The authors of Transformative Innovation in Education put it this way:

If you spend all your time protecting the Rocks of the status quo in Horizon One then you risk becoming a dinosaur, isolated as the world sails by. But spend all your time thrashing about in the Whirlpools of Third Horizon innovations then people might perceive you and your ideas a little bit like Scotland's national animal, the Unicorn – magical, mysterious but leaving people never quite sure whether the ideas become reality, never quite sure whether they can take you seriously. A balance between the two is where innovation lies: creative ideas that borrow from the heritage of the organisation's founding values.

The process the authors then suggest takes innovation teams on a to-and-fro journey between these sometimes contradictory Rock and Whirlpool Values, to better understand the potential conflict that might arise, the grey, predictable compromises one might make, and leave space to begin to reconsider how our ideas might evolve further to become not only audacious, but more likely to succeed within the organisation.

It is what my team call a 'pre-mortem' – post-mortems are less useful in innovation projects, as the idea is, by then, dead beyond revival. A pre-mortem is a period of safe reflection to consider all the potential causes for the future death of our idea and give us a chance to take some preventative measures to alter our ideas, and make them more likely to thrive in the real world.

Rock Values – what values are revealed in the First Horizon?

In Transformative Innovation in Education, the authors argue that innovations we develop in The Third Horizon rarely find their feet because the very problems we observed in the status quo of Horizon One exist, in part, due to the underlying values of the organisation, values that will not move fast.

If these values will not change swiftly, then innovation will take longer to take its place in the organisation, if it manages to take its place at all. They refer to these values as sturdy, steady 'Rock Values'. The metaphor of Rocks has sometimes been interpreted by innovation teams as 'blocks', but Rocks needn't (and invariably should not) be perceived as negative. Very often, none of us want to get rid of these Rock Values because they offer useful things to us all: accountability, comparability, transparency, and so on.

These Rock Values will be vital to the success, on the ground, of the innovation we have developed in the Third Horizon, since the people we are trying to engage with the innovation, the people we are trying to help better, have these values engrained in the way they currently operate and think about the organisation. Their very sense of belonging is tied up in those Rock Values.

In educator workshops, we've found that when people

are asked what the 'Rock Values' of their institution might be, we get a list of a dozen values that sound like any other school's, regardless of culture, country or the type of school undertaking the task: caring for all, excellence, accountability, research-led, student-centred. We can add much more value, and sincerity, to these values if we dig into the actual observations and discoveries made during the immersive phase of the First Horizon.

When we do this, we discover more difference between institutions. Many Rock Values are the positive ones that school leaders would have cited on being asked for them in the first place, but others, less visible in the day-to-day bustle of school or formal strategy document, are important to bear in mind when we're trying to create change and innovate.

For example, in one university a key value was 'honouring language, culture and identity' of the large number of different students' backgrounds. Other values were 'cultural intelligence', making connections and co-creation. These were found within the actual goings-on at the school, even though the 'formal' Rock Values were much more predictable: meeting budgets, teaching and learning, striving for excellence, and so on.

Separating these Rock Values (values that we know exist today, in the First Horizon) from the Whirlpool Values (values we aspire to innovate towards) makes discussion about the ideas we have already generated much clearer: just to what extent will the innovation team have to alter behaviour to make this work? One team at a New Zealand school put it this way:

'We talked about the process and how it worked by getting the internalised thoughts out there first. They told me that the way it was developed (as pieces not as a whole) meant that if they made a statement they were challenged about where it belonged, "Is that a whirlpool or maybe that belongs in the rock segment?" and this was great.'

In another example, Andrée Marcotte, an educator

from Laurentides in rural Quebec, noted that her local schools would probably cite the slightly predictable 'integrity, transparency, recognising everyone' as Rock Values. But she also discovered through the process that there was a key value innovators might glance over: good timing.

In her case, she realised that even a great innovation with exciting Whirlpool Values will still fail, according to her team's analysis, if the timing during a busy school year doesn't quite work for the whole staff.

In short, we can test each other's assumptions about what values actually exist today (Rock Values) and what values we aspire to (Whirlpool Values). If we aspire to a new, Whirlpool Value, then the ideas we generate have to bring about the necessary change to help that value take its place, eventually, amongst the institution's Rock Values.

We can't just magic up that change.

Whirlpool Values – the innovative qualities of nascent Third Horizon ideas

The Third Horizon innovations that we have just created are, in their early days, often perceived by the majority of folk as the nautical counterpoint of Rocks – Whirlpools.

Whirlpools are exciting, for sure, but also potentially risky, something you can get stuck in. In the same way as a Rock Value is neither good nor bad – it's just a value that exists consistently in the status quo of Horizon One – the Whirlpool Values of our innovation are not necessarily always 'good'. That excitement can also be destabilising for people. The taking of a risk, while often celebrated by leaders, is normally the antithesis of the value evoked by that same leader's five-year plan – everything laid out, in advance, to the nth degree.

A group of schools in New Zealand had been through various processes already to develop ideas to solve problems they had noticed for some time, but there was a problem with this ongoing innovation. An innovation workshop leader described the challenge faced by this group: 'We talked about the creative solutions that we had written on the [workshop] day. We knew these were mostly things we'd already thought about over the year but hadn't recorded anywhere.' This comment stresses the importance of an innovation team maintaining a Project Nest from Horizon One, even into the later stages of idea and vision development in Horizon Three.

We need to have the evidence in front of us, to sense check whether the ideas we are generating are going to require a little, a lot or an unsurmountable level of change in the values of those in our learning communities. And, to understand that evidence fully, we need plenty of time to digest it, not just a single innovation workshop awayday.

The New Zealand facilitator continues, showing us the importance of taking time over this Horizon One synthesis process: 'I started writing the comments around the page a couple of days after we did the session, I had had time to think and make connections. I found myself thinking of things, then looking at the rock values to check if they belonged. This helped a lot.'

From the hundreds of ideas developed in the Third Horizon, what are the key values they exemplify? What are the connections between those ideas, what values bind them? For example, at Rosendale Primary School, in south London, United Kingdom, we were keen to give students more visibility of their progress in learning, and had developed several ideas that harnessed laptops, iPads and small touch devices.

The values behind such ideas included portability, providing personal devices for personal reflections, speedy switch-on of the device, the ability to capture a learning reflection in more than just text, but by camera, audio or video, the excitement of being able to use technology more regularly in one's learning.

We asked ourselves: Are there any tensions or conflicts in the values between those ideas? Are there any obvious tensions or conflicts between the Whirlpool Values of the ideas proposed for the Third Horizon and the Rock Values we have already identified from the here-and-now of the First Horizon? In this regard, some of our initial Third Horizon ideas had values that were in conflict with the values of the school.

First of all, budget: we had no access to technology that we needed, and staff professional development on its use hadn't been planned or budgeted for either.

Second there were conflicts in the values between some of our ideas: we wanted students to have a personal means of recording their reflection, but some of our ideas still relied on the teacher recording the evidence of student progress.

It is these differences that will fuel the next step with this tool: undertaking a pre-mortem, as we run through all the potential conflicts our Whirlpool Values might encounter with the Rock Values that underpin our institution today.

Pre-mortem: Imagining The Conflict

Conflict needn't be a bad thing, and in the creative industries is often part and parcel of developing great fresh ideas. We talk about 'creative conflict' as a means of working out the blemishes on a good idea to turn it into a great idea. It is unlikely that any new idea will ever be accepted by every constituent as perfect and palatable.

Yet, this inevitable conflict can lead to a new idea being squashed before it's had a chance to fully develop. When the conflicts are less seismic but nonetheless persistent, the result is often visible in symptoms such as repeated non-committal meetings, where people walk around ideas endlessly, but nothing ever comes of them. Endless nagging conflict results in innovation becoming nothing more than a series of talking shops.

As the authors of Transformative Innovation in Education put it, the team ends up the animal equivalent of another mystical creature, Dr Doolittle's Pushme-Pullme, as innovators thinking exclusively about the Third Horizon, the creative space of the future pull one way, and those living the day-to-day of the moment, in the established status quo, in the First Horizon, adhering to the comfortable, familiar Rock Values, pull the other.

The potential for stagnation can be avoided by identifying all the potential conflicts which may arise between Whirlpool Values from the creative ideas of the Third Horizon and the Rock Values of the First Horizon.

In a workshop setting, we ask people to quite literally quote the phrases that will be uttered as and when people hear of the innovation team's nascent ideas.

These are some real (predictable) examples:

'We have different needs'
'This isn't what I was employed to do'
'There are no systems in place to cope with this'
'I don't have the confidence'
'I don't have the training to do this'
'I don't want to look needy'
'It's alright for the others, they know how to do it'
'Squeaky wheels get the oil...'
'I don't have the time; I'm too busy on [the old way of doing things]'

Stating these for all to see is often a light point in building one's strategy, a realisation that, indeed, many members of the innovation team have or would have said the same kind of thing.

Each phrase in turn leads to a decision: if we heard that piece of conflict, how might we adapt our idea to meet the point the person is making?

That design decision, that change in the ideas you've developed already in the Third Horizon, can go one of two ways: a creative resolution that actually improves the original ideas, or a grey compromise that neither achieves the Whirlpool Values of the innovators nor meets in the long term the Rock Values of the organisation.

Avoiding Grey Compromises

Unfortunately, many innovation teams fall for a grey compromise, that is, a compromise that fails to both promote the Rock Values of the organisation and protect those Whirlpool Values that made the innovative idea so innovative in the first place. For example, one-to-one computer rollouts in schools were deemed highly innovative throughout the early 2000s, and today in many environments and cultures the once Whirlpool Value of 'every child has access to a personal computer' is now a firm Rock Value, untouchable, not subject to negotiation.

In the United Kingdom, access to broadband, seen as a luxury to many barely five years ago, is now considered by Government as being as important a utility as electricity, gas or water. Yet even this, an apparent logic to many, has failed to stick in other environments:

Some school systems that ushered in one-to-one laptop programs amid great fanfare have begun to scrap them because of budget cuts (Lemagie, 2010); mushrooming maintenance costs (Vascellaro, 2006); and concerns about how students are using the computers (Hu, 2007).

Many district leaders continue to believe that one-to-one programs are worth the expense and headaches.

Why do some school leaders see laptop programs as scrappable, while others see them as being worth the expense and headaches, as important utilities for learning?

The answer is obvious with hindsight – there's not enough budget to pay for maintenance, for student and staff development in how to harness them responsibly for learning. Had these three elements been brought together in a pre-mortem, we might have designed our laptop programs from the start with far more budget and time allocated for the very elements which would, if left untended, spell an end to the innovation.

It is also possible for a grey compromise to end up

safeguarding solely the values of the innovative idea: the lone innovator teacher getting on with things in their classroom but not seeing their ideas replicated across school is a prime example. In the short term it gives the innovator a thrill to see their ideas play out, but in the long term it's a failure, creating resentment and ill-feeling from the 'have nots' who haven't been able to benefit from the innovation going on there.

Most often, it is the Rock Values that tend to win the day, forcing otherwise Whirlpool Values down into the corner of grey compromise, where the very innovative Whirlpools we sought are watered down beyond all recognition. To pick up the one-to-one laptop example once more, a one-to-one tablet program is an innovative idea, but perhaps balancing the budget is cited as a key priority for the school. The grey compromise here is creating a one-to-one laptop program, for a few classes, using older technologies. It might appear to some as achieving what the innovator was setting out to do, but longer term it's not, and could, in fact, set back other innovations on the same theme. The animal metaphor applied by the Transformative Innovation in Education team is one of the ostrich with its head in the sand.

A New Zealand facilitator has used this specific technique with schools with whom she is working. The feedback from her teachers shows the impact of breaking down the assumptions and making them clear for all through such a process:

They all felt that this worked because you got the crap out of the way first. Those thoughts that are hiding normally are acknowledged and accepted as being there and real. But by exposing them, you can't hide behind them any more, and you can't use the excuse and get away with it. This chart is going on their wall and others will have a chuckle when someone strays into the compromise area.

Creative Resolutions – Redefining, Reshaping, Rewriting Ideas

You've mapped out the Rock Values that emerge from your research in the First Horizon, and you're keenly aware of the Whirlpool Values that make your innovative idea innovative in the first place. You've gone on to look at the potential conflicts that might arise, in your 'pre-mortem', and have also identified what you would not want your idea to become, were it to be compromised as a result of each of those potential conflicts.

The task that remains now, is to reframe your original ideas as something that meets the potential conflicts that may arise, but which gives equal billing to both the Rock Values that are vital and the Whirlpool Values that generate the much-needed solution to the problem you've been working on.

This final element of this tool is the Second Horizon, the heavy-lifting that gets us to the audacious goals we set out in the Third Horizon. Working out that route to success helps our ideas to 'soar like an eagle', if we are to continue the animal metaphors from Leicester et al. It is likely that this continued development of our ideas does not take place in the same design session during which we've 'danced the dilemma dance'. It is a significant creative venture that is required.

As our New Zealand consultant pointed out from the end of her session: 'Without thinking, they all realised this was going to need collaboration on a big scale to make it work. These guys work in silos – 4 walls, 1 teacher, 30 kids. It was like an epiphany, everyone suggested working in groups, having staff and team meetings, supporting each other, leaning on experts... A really solid outcome from this group who traditionally play it very safe and stick to what they know.'

NEXT STEPS IN IDEATION: LET THE JUICES FLOW

- ✓ Keep ambition high – Third Horizon vision is not about feasibility, but audaciousness.
- ✓ If you spot big opportunities for ideas, go back and seek out small details too. Big and small together lead to great ideas.
- ✓ Try to resist killing ideas on feasibility alone – if the idea is the best at solving the problem you've identified, the team will find a way to make it happen.
- ✓ Quantity over quality is the attitude required to find a gem of an idea.
- ✓ Resist the 'but' – stick with 'yes, and...' as long as possible. Add to each other's ideas. Don't destroy them.
- ✓ Can you work out what you're competing against? What is up against any of your ideas succeeding? How do they differentiate themselves from the status quo? Are you creating something that will be easier to take up than continuing with the status quo?
- ✓ What will people throw up against your idea? Can you use this to redefine the idea, improve it for all by making it accessible to everyone?

THE SECOND HORIZON – GETTING THERE

'If you have an apple and I have an apple and we exchange these apples then you and I will still each have one apple. But if you have an idea and I have an idea and we exchange these ideas, then each of us will have two ideas.'
George Bernard Shaw

Ewan McIntosh

PROTOTYPING CULTURE

You may not have yet settled on the precise phrasing of your big hairy audacious goal of the Third Horizon, but you probably have a clear enough idea of what the solution to your problem is that you need to start redesigning it around the practicalities of the environment around you. That journey, from the First Horizon status quo to the Third Horizon big vision, is called The Second Horizon.

At a basic level, when this part of the innovation begins is a question of good timing. All too often, startups and school innovators alike unveil their fully-polished, ready-to-launch idea far too late in the day. They've coded the last line, they've printed the policy document in full colour, they've made a... wait for it... PowerPoint presentation to explain how it's all going to work. They've effectively built a full-fat, heavy idea that has little chance of hopping from the innovator team's interests across the chasm to the more mainstream audience.

More successful startups cross this chasm several times, back and forth, with much smaller more nimble ideas that people can take on board, understand, internalise and put into action in their own lives or classrooms, without too much pain. Better still, any pain they do feel using that idea early on can be captured and fed back into the next version of the idea when it crosses the chasm in the weeks to come.

This back-and-forth route to the Third Horizon is as much cultural as process-driven. It is a culture of prototyping that has to be nurtured, encouraged and stimulated by example from the leadership team.

A prototype is a working model of a solution. Prototyping is a great way of quickly showing the people you involved in the immersion and empathy stage that you've done something with their hard effort. It's also a great way to test ideas. In the classroom, it's one of the principal places formative, peer-to-peer and self-assessment is illustrated in totally concrete (or post-it, or papier maché) terms.

The prototype is not the final version, and ideally this whole process would lead to several prototypes aiming to solve the same problem. Small groups might siphon off into pairs or individuals developing prototypes and then coming together to share their work before then all developing the best prototype into a full working product. This swift reflective iterative process in the world of startups is called rapid prototyping, typified by an openness to receive feedback and use it to change the original idea. There is a lack of defensiveness over ideas we've been developing; we are rarely that precious about an original idea since we've not been holding onto it long enough to develop that kind of steady relationship with it.

The first versions of your idea might be nothing more than a sketch and a short dialogue by way of introduction – just enough to get some feedback. A second iteration might require the idea to be 'made'. And everything can be made physical.

In 2013, NoTosh worked with a large British telecommunications company, with the goal to shine a light on innovation coming from employees working at the coalface day in, day out. The results were fabulous. In the course of one week of workshops around the country, employees generated over 700 ideas to improve the business.

Most of them were about systems, about the way people interact with other people and the services on offer.

How To Come Up With Great Ideas and Actually Make Them Happen

They weren't physical fixes, they were cultural or intellectual ones.

When the staff were invited to 'build' their idea, using a host of craft materials and the ubiquitous LEGO bricks, their reaction was one of incredulity. Yet, in a brief 10-minute prototyping session, most had built something that helped them explain incredibly complex systems in totally clear terms to people who worked in different departments, without prior technical knowledge. Making their idea made it tangible and comprehensible. Furthermore, the fact that their LEGO and craft material models were playful and child-like in their look, they were also unthreatening.

People were able to really listen in full, without immediately coming to conclusions about what it was they were being shown or having their mind taken up with defensive questions on how this new idea might affect them. The atmosphere was more one of laughter than analysis, yet the result was stronger analysis than in many formal meetings on innovative ideas the teams had had before.

In the past, when new ideas were presented in plush polished PowerPoint files, backed up with lots of figures, members of staff felt that the decision to innovate on such or such a thing had already been taken: so much work had been put into the presentation that it was, they felt, too late to chime in with their own feedback on how this might actually work, on the ground. This time around, though, the quality of feedback was better than it had normally been when similar ideas had been presented in the past: no one had spent more than 10 minutes creating the model, the slightly weird-looking collection of LEGO models proved that, and so no one felt too guilty about giving honest feedback and critique of what they were being shown.

You don't always have to build your idea with LEGO bricks, though. Amazon's innovation approach, which it calls 'working backwards', has hinged on prototyping since its early days as a startup. Its product managers begin any project by writing an internal press release announcing the finished product, forcing themselves to be concise about the benefit to their customers. So, learning institutions might also consider a prototype of the newsletter to parents or alumni, or the video from the Head Teacher for the website.

The key is not to build something of studio or journalistic integrity – it is to build in the least amount of time with the least amount of money a version of the idea that communicates its most important elements. This balance of creating an idea that is just 'good enough', and no more, is core to prototyping culture. Senior leaders often feel foolish translating their big hairy ambitious goals into such small, playful, diminutive models. They often say that it simplifies the complexities of their grand idea. They hint that with barely ten minutes to build their idea, the idea cannot possibly be considered valid enough to actually share. Rotman Professor Roger Martin argues the opposite on this question of what constitutes 'good enough':

> *Validity is what might be right, even if it's not been proven before. Reliability is what has been proven in the past to work (but whose future is just as uncertain in a time of flux). A growth mindset, where a person constantly learns and relearns in order to survive and thrive requires validity over reliability, knowing that deadends and failure can be learned from to create successes for the longer term benefit of the organisation.*

'Companies are good at producing 'hothouse tomatoes', says John Maeda... 'Perfectly formed and identical, edible but not delicious. Most don't yet know how to integrate the "heirloom tomato", the tomato that looks a little different from the rest, lovingly grown by hand with attention to detail, mouthwateringly delicious.'

The difference between ideas that feel valid today versus

those that will be truly valid tomorrow is a fine one. And the only way to make the small changes that result, over time, in the big change, that move from the hothouse tomato to the heirloom tomato, is to prototype, early and often, and feed off the feedback you seek out. This is more than a project strategy.

To have the greatest effect, everyone in the organisation has to believe in the potential of unfinished, part-ready, messy prototypes, and know their role in giving quality feedback to make them better.

QUALITY FEEDBACK

Soliciting feedback
The techniques for soliciting and giving quality feedback on an early prototype are not dissimilar to those we might employ in an effective classroom. In fact, many of those in the technology and creative industries would stand to benefit from emulating techniques already employed in their local schools. You might follow Ron Berger's advice on asking for 'Kind, Specific, and Useful' feedback, or harness a simple technique like 'Two stars and a wish', where those giving you feedback must provide two elements they like and one element that is up for improvement.

In every case, we want to seek useful feedback with some indications, perhaps, of what exactly the giver of feedback might do differently – do they have a suggestion of how we might overcome the shortfall they identified? We must listen to all feedback, especially suggestions for improvement, with a healthy pinch of salt, and we must, always, go back to the evidence in our project nest from the First Horizon, and the Whirlpool Values we identified around our innovative idea in the Third Horizon, to test feedback against what we felt we had known.

Feedback from peers is useful. The environment for doing this can be more helpful than a board meeting. At

Google X Labs, the highly secretive research and development lab for the technology giant, the innovation team will take one person's idea and then everyone goes about trying to build prototypes of that. It means that the individual failures or shortcomings of each and every prototype inform the business decision that is taken next: do we pursue this right now down a different angle, do more homework in our First Horizon to test that our assumptions are correct, or do we put this on the back burner for the time being until we are able to come by more information, budget or time?

Having more than one prototype under production by more than one team at any one time means that the team is able to reach failure faster, cheaper and with less heartache – they've not had that much time to become emotionally attached to their idea. They hold their ideas lightly. The physical prototypes they build are, in fact, the prime 'giver' of feedback. They don't need people to tell them whether their thermo-acoustic engine concept is going to solve the world's energy crises. Their version of the idea, made from hardware store resources, gives them plenty of direction in what works, what is likely to be problematic if this idea is pursued further.

Using feedback
This need for participants in the design or innovation team to use that feedback, to admit that they have failed, is tough to achieve. How we receive feedback is as important as how we solicit it. 'The process of innovation is messy, it's expensive, it's uncertain. Even with Google X and the resources we have here we can only afford to pursue a small number of these moonshots at a time,' says Google X Rapid Evaluation Team Lead Rich DeVaul. 'We therefore try to fail quickly. In a day or two, let's do some experiments that give us an idea about how feasible that is. Ultimately, if we can get to a "no" quickly on an idea, that's almost as good as getting to a "yes".'

Google X's Astro Teller has been known to hug employees who admit that they have failed in their project. 'Most people come hardwired, trained by society, that if they don't do the thing that they said they were going to do, if it doesn't come out bright, shiny and sparkly, that someone is going to get mad at them. Everyone is like that the day they start with us. The question is whether they have the desire within them to unlearn that, to get to the place – after 50 or 100 hugs – where they'll believe us when we say 'Hey it broke, it didn't work? Awesome! Did we learn anything out of that, is there anything we shouldn't do again?'

In short, it's preferable that they realise early that their idea is a poor fit, than later, when the company has invested more than just their salaries in their latest idea.

Prototyping in the real world

You might wish to take the notion of prototyping further. Often, people show prototypes to people like them or, if they manage to get to a wider spread of potential users of their idea, the prototype is experienced out of context in a focus group or team discussion. In other cases, organisations look at the data emerging from the use of a prototype, and make decisions based on the data jumping off the screen.

Paul Graham, startup mentor and internet entrepreneur, puts forward the most important advice for those creating prototypes of their idea: 'Go meet the people.'

This kind of human interaction is not very large scale, and not comprehensive, but the information gleaned from taking the prototype out to real people in the real world is far more informative for the developing idea.

Taking the earliest version of a prototype out into the real world is something many product designers are beginning to do, to see how it performs in the real natural habitat they would like it to one day inhabit. Tom Hulme,

Design Director of IDEO in London, talks about where this desire to test in the real world comes from:

The power of social media and television programmes such as Dragons' Den [also known as Shark Tank] may have even increased our fear of public humiliation from failure in business.

But there is an alternative: instead of soliciting feedback from customers in focus groups, which we all know never really mimic real life, why not try placing the prototype in its real context?

Walter Faulstroh did just this. When co-launching V Water, a soft drink that was subsequently acquired by Pepsi, he took a prototype of the product and placed it on supermarket shelves without asking for permission from the retailer.

After watching if passing shoppers ignored or picked it up, he would ask them why. The in-market feedback was faster and higher quality because the context was real.

Social media are making it even easier to release prototypes to a wide number of users. Zynga, the social gaming developer, goes public even before it has written a line of code. It prioritises new game concepts by creating a five-word pitch for each and advertising it on a high-traffic website of relevant users.

If the pitch is clicked on, the user is diverted to a survey that harvests e-mails and additional information. Zynga then compares interest for each pitch and prioritises accordingly. The company calls this approach 'ghetto testing' and it guarantees an excited market before launch, lowering the chance of most entrepreneurs' greatest fear: market rejection.

In the education world, we can see this notion of testing ideas in the real world being played out on crowdfunding websites such as Kickstarter. Two students from the MFA Interaction Design program at the School of Visual Arts (SVA), NYC, decided in early 2014 to write a book, The Maker's Alphabet, to explain the multitude of possibilities of craft, electronics, computer programming and making to children 'aged 1-100'.

The traditional concept would have languished in a publisher's in-tray for months before, probably, being refused – two unpublished authors, students at that, with no proven 'expertise' in the domain, trying to head into a Red Ocean of competition in the Maker book space.

Yet, with a target of $4500, Melody Quintana and Sneha Pai managed to garner nearly three times that by the time their deadline came up, and continue to take orders for the book through the site. How did they do it? They prototyped their ideas for some of the panels in the book simply, cheaply and pulled together a powerful story in video form for the Kickstarter website. The moment they pressed 'publish' on their Kickstarter video and mockups for the book, they hit feedback listening mode, hearing what their 348 backers were telling them, and nuancing their idea as a result. They even invite backers to have a say in how they define the letter 'X' of The Maker's Alphabet!

They were sharing their prototypes in the real world, for all to see. People could have hated it, but at least they wouldn't have invested $4500 of their own money in a dumb idea. Instead, they are reaping the benefits of prototyping 'live', in the real world, and generating support for the idea in the process, as more and more people feel they are part of something special.

Beware Partners

Testing your idea with a crowdfunding site is one option. Many use such services not so much for the cash they can receive but for the feedback a successful funding drive (or an unsuccessful one) gives them. There is a difference, therefore, between using a crowdfunding site (primarily for feedback) and appealing for resources within a school, district, university or Foundation fund.

Paul Graham, a long-standing internet entrepreneur, venture capitalist and startup adviser, is, ironically, wary of startups who seek to 'partner' with a bigger organisation early on. Big organisations might offer cash, personnel and their 'brand' to help your idea grow, but they come with all sorts of other inhibitors as you develop your nascent idea into something longer term:

Partnerships too usually don't work. They don't work for startups in general, but they especially don't work as a way to get growth started. It's a common mistake among inexperienced founders to believe that a partnership with a big company will be their big break. Six months later they're all saying the same thing: that was way more work than we expected, and we ended up getting practically nothing out of it.

In the manual Business Model Generation, the distinction made between Partners and Customers is polar: partners can rarely become your customers, and they are placed at opposite sides of the planning tool provided so that the stark difference is clear.

Indeed, partnering with an organisation, even just in return for the apparent kudos it might lend your idea, can end up holding you back in the longer term, or changing your idea for the worse due to the partner's assumption that they have some sway over your emergent ideas.

For a startup, this might mean that the large tech company who offer their brand and network to spread your concept, app or service will rarely give up the free access they enjoy to your idea to become a paying customer.

In education terms, a school that is developing an idea which benefits, say, parents the most might think of partnering with the Parent Teachers Association for all sorts of reasons – partnering brings legitimacy to the idea, the insights of the PTA members or their network of influence on the parent community. On the flip side, the PTA may start to introduce their own biases to the mix, during this Second Horizon. We might know that their biases are unfounded from the research we've undertaken in the First Horizon, and we might have spotted their potential conflict in our analysis of the Third Horizon idea we have started to develop but, as a partner, the PTA might feel its opinion has more weight than the 'random' broad research you have done in the First Horizon. As a result, politics gets in the way of a good idea developing swiftly.

The lesson? By all means make sure in the case above that you include the PTA in your First Horizon investigations and even in your Third Horizon ideation, but as you enter the prototyping phase of the Second Horizon, don't take their feedback with any more weight than the next individual parent, student or teacher.

Don't assume that partnering is going to make a healthy difference to the end product. For innovation, often, the early days are best walked alone, with your innovation team.

STORYBOARDING FROM STRATEGY TO JOURNEY

After the feedback from the initial prototypes you create, there comes a point where one needs to move beyond the physical artefact, and start seeing where the process fits into the whole context. We need to see the bigger picture, and how our idea fits in it. We need to get feedback from people on what that journey feels like. Is that journey best expressed in a five-year strategy document, resplendent in 50 or more pages, destined never to be read by anyone outside the leadership suite?

Storyboarding over the past 90 or so years has been how filmmakers have made a connection between the script and the final experience. So why not leaders, too, wanting to make the script of their strategy turn, quickly, into pragmatic action on the ground?

AirBnB is a service that matches people needing a place to stay with private individuals who have a room, apartment or a whole house to rent out for a few days or weeks. The service had a very start-stop beginning in its life, struggling to get funding, and struggling to get people coming back to use the service again, or tell their friends to use it. With this block, founder Joe Gebbia encouraged everyone in his team to draw their idea of what the service's strongest points were, those memorable moments. His belief, like many other users of storyboards, is that if you can draw your idea, then other people will be able to picture it, too, understand it, take part in it far better than if it stays in abstract, two-dimensional form.

Rather than just one sketch or one built prototype, Gebbia harnesses the power of the storyboard to get people thinking like Experience Architects, thinking through the idea from the moment someone finds out the idea exists, through to their success in using it, taking part in it, or getting some kind of benefit out of it. The storyboard is a key tool in turning a theoretically interesting two-dimensional idea, or three-dimensional physical prototype, into a 'four-dimensional' pragmatic experience in the real world that benefits people.

In 2012, with AirBnB needing to revisit its model and reexamine every step of the experience, the entire team turned to storyboarding. They drew out what their version of success felt like, what their ideas looked like as they entered the world, who was there with them as it happened, what role they were playing in making that success happen. Gebbia storyboarded himself, standing at the door with a big welcome mat on the floor, three airbeds on the ground with a mint on each pillow. He pictured himself as a host. This picturing of success, and thinking through the personal contributions required by each member of the team to make that innovation happen, was key to gaining more empathy with the customer. It helped the entire team understand what might be required to make perfect each type of experience by each type of person on the service. Drawing what it feels like shows the details that will make the big hairy audacious goal become a reality.

Bernard Otabil, an entrepreneur running a non-profit in Ghana with whom we worked in 2011, was struck by the power of creating a storyboard for his service. His mobile phone service helps rural farmers in Ghana generate more revenue by working more effectively. 'Building a persona and storyboard really helped bridge the relationship between our team, the innovators, and what we're trying to do,' he said. 'What we've developed, will it really be useful for the end user? What kind of improvements will it need to get that out of the product? All those questions come through periods of disagreement, punching holes in what we had spent so much time doing.'

MAINTAINING CREATIVITY WITH FEASIBILITY

The Second Horizon is often viewed as the pragmatic edge of the process. The First Horizon is an opportunity to dip into the current state of affairs, satisfying and 'safe' as we deal with the knowledge we acquire through the process. The Third Horizon is viewed as the most creative opportunity to develop ideas that solve the problems raised in the First Horizon. The Second Horizon, surely, is where the hackles come down and reality brings those ideas back down to earth? Not entirely. The role of innovation leader in balancing the creative edge we have gained through the Third Horizon and the pragmatism of the Second Horizon is crucial.

As a case in point, we can see how creativity and success never ceases to thrive in the world-famous Cirque du Soleil. This global franchise is a hugely successful business: it generates $700m annually, with 13 shows in four continents. There are shows in 250 cities in the world, with permanent shows in Las Vegas that have been complemented with permanent shows in Asia.

But it is an organisation that came not from the corridors of a business school, but from the 'school of the street', as Cirque du Soleil CEO Daniel Lamarre puts it. From a band of street performers, the Cirque du Soleil is known for consistently innovating its offering, avoiding the risk of being typecast as 'just another circus'. Its Third Horizon goal – to invoke the imagination, provoke the senses and evoke the emotions of people around the world – is as ambitious and audacious as one might get. But the route to get there, its Second Horizon, is marked by several ever-changing ways of working, and a huge degree of trust and delegation to a finely tuned innovation motor.

For example, the Cirque has no animal shows, a choice made to differentiate itself from the other entertainment offerings out there. Its creative process is marked by both the huge creativity that one sees in the performances, and a laser-sharp specificity that comes with the clarity of their Third Horizon the 'flavour' that makes the Cirque so immediately recognisable and the processes they use to make that Third Horizon happen. An internal group, the 'trend group', feeds the artistic directors with new trends they spot on their travels around the world. Fifty scouts travel the world to find the best artists of the moment. Seven thousand performers are on the Cirque's books, meaning that, with this data, they have huge analytical tools to help the creative directors create new shows that one would not see anywhere else.

There is a highly distinct formula with the Cirque du Soleil which can be shared with this huge number of people, driven by data on the one hand and artistic freedom of its directors on the other. Those investing in the ideas are third parties, and have no influence on the creative teams. They have no need: as long as the Cirque continues to meet its Third Horizon mission, to invoke the imagination, provoke the senses and evoke the emotions of its audiences, those leaders are happy. How the innovation teams get there is down to them, and them alone. By having creative cells like these, the Cirque can protect the artistic integrity of its teams. The trust and confidence of the investors and leaders comes from the knowledge that creative decisions are based on an immersion in this ever-updated set of data delivered by scouts, the trend group and the skills and experiences of the creative teams.

EXPLAINING (AND CHANGING) YOUR IDEAS

The Second Horizon is typified by a nervousness about when to commit to the prototype in more than small iterations but to really go for it, and seeking investment of one's colleagues or, in some cases, actual investment of cash or resources from a leadership team, finance officer, board or Foundation fund. Yet, one of the biggest mistakes you can make as an innovator is explaining your idea too late, or too concretely. Explaining your idea to colleagues or parents after an 'extensive period of development' might sound to some like preparedness, but it actually puts your audience on the back foot – it's too late for them to do anything about it, they have no say over your idea, they will never 'own' it. The prototyping culture which has informed your journey so far has to continue even as the innovation team begins to have overwhelming confidence in the idea around which they are planning.

SOCIALISE YOUR IDEAS EARLY
You may have placed some simple prototypes out in the wild to see how 'real people' use them, or to gauge people's reactions to your new ideas. Or, if the idea feels too young to put out there, you may have tested the idea by building it, or soliciting feedback from your internal innovation team colleagues. But there is another group of people who can provide incredibly useful feedback on early ideas: your peers.

How To Come Up With Great Ideas and Actually Make Them Happen

Most startup entrepreneurs are part of the wider community of people like them. That doesn't mean that they turn up at the same institution, nine-to-five, get a job done and go home, with maybe the occasional pint with the work team. Startup entrepreneurs live and breathe their idea to almost insane levels: they talk about it, share it, as early as the first moments they have it. They go to pitching events to share it formally with investors, although rarely is there realistic thought that the investment will come that early on – they want feedback, and they want their ideas socialised.

There is an inherent risk in sharing your idea early, a risk that is nearly always unfounded – 'If I show my idea early, then someone might steal it'. Tech entrepreneurs, however, often turn up informal BarCamp events to share their ideas with people who could, in theory, build something similar themselves. Most folk now recognise this in the Hollywood treatment of the Winklevoss twins, who shared their idea with Mark Zuckerberg and were convinced that his competitive idea of 'The Facebook' was a carbon copy. Most of the time, startups are too busy building their own ideas to care about stealing other people's. They're already convinced that they have found the problem that needed solving. But what they can all provide each other is that capacity to start a creative conflict about the 'right' way to tackle any given challenge, the 'best' way to code your way out of it.

This creative conflict, and having a specified time, place and expectation of vibrant, rough discussion, has been around for centuries, along with the threat that someone could 'rip off' one's ideas. Michael P. Farrell describes how the Impressionists got their act together and, through collective creative conflict every week, were able to produce individually brilliant work, without necessarily exposing themselves to the risk of having their nascent ideas stolen. In fact, what he describes shows the huge value in having informed peers critique ideas early on:

By 1869, the Impressionist group had established the ritual of meeting on Thursday nights at Café Guerbois at 11 rue des Batignolles. They had two tables where they met just inside the door on the left. Their area was separated from the rest of the café by a glass partition... In an interview about the café period of his life, Claude Monet reports:

> *'It wasn't until 1860 that I saw Manet again, but we became close friends at once, as soon as we met. He invited me to come and see him each evening in the café in the Batignolle district where he and his friends met when the day's work in the studio was over. There I met... Cézanne, Degas who had just returned from a trip to Italy, the art critic Duranty, Emile Zola who was then making his debut in literature, and several others as well. I myself brought along Sisley, Bazille, and Renoir. Nothing could be more interesting than the talks we had with their perpetual clashes of opinion. Your mind was held in suspense all the time, you spurred the others on to sincere, disinterested inquiry and were spurred on yourself, you laid in a stock of enthusiasm that kept you going for weeks on end until you could give final form the idea you had in mind. You always went home afterwards better shelled for the fray, with a new sense of purpose and a clearer head.' (Cited from Denvir 1990, 74)*

This, to me, sounds like an artistic TeachMeet, although the regularity of the group, the critical conversations and overarching projects and idea development that brew behind the discussion are more akin to something from the startup world of today: Coffee Mornings. In the Spring of 2006, I sat in a booth with Michael Coulter, an advertising copywriter of repute, and no more than four others.

Mike had brought the group together as 'Edinburgh Coffee Morning', using his blog to send out the word. He had heard about one the previous week in London by another adman, Russell Davies.

The idea is that, every week, at the same time in the same café, creative people can get together and talk about their projects, work through their vision and maybe get an insight into how to solve their current challenge. And sometimes you end up having had just a good coffee and a catchup with friends.

But the creative essence of the Impressionists' café community lives on in startup culture now, the world over, through regular creative mornings, coffee mornings or weekly tech meetups. Regularity, dispassionate passion for creative ideas, critical friends to give you an honest idea, and trust that your failures are safe.

In schools, though, it's rare to find a weekly forum for such creative conflict, and so the habit has a hard time forming. The weekly staff meeting is, in most places, not the ideal environment for this kind of jovial, dispassionate creative conflict.

There are 'important' things being discussed, action points that take precedence before 'nice ideas for the future'.

Some schools buck the trend. In rural Queensland, in the village of Boonah, Head Teacher Phillip Manitta has started to hold the weekly staff meeting in a different teacher's classroom every week.

In their 'café' they are the boss, so they lead the start of the meeting for 15 minutes, sharing what ideas they've been developing, and another 15 minutes are spent in discussion about how colleagues might develop that idea further, were it them leading the class.

The onus is not on 'pleasant' feedback – it's on pragmatic improvement.

And most weeks the meeting might well lend itself better to a café, as it's a struggle moving staff away from creative conflict onto the more mundane matters of regular school administration and Getting Things Done.

ACTOR MAPPING – STRATEGY BUILT AROUND PEOPLE

As we develop our ideas for the Third Horizon, we are already segmenting the 'audiences' who will benefit from the idea. In particular, with the Beachhead mapped out, we can see not only the segments we will appeal to, but also the subsequent groups we will move onto as the concept develops over time.

The beachhead helps us prioritise who we will approach first. An actor mapping exercise helps us work out what potential nuance in the idea will be required for each group in our community.

This exercise constitutes yet another prototype, as simply the process of thinking through the relationships involved and the biases that creep in provide useful feedback that informs a redesign, or the creation of a new idea.

All too often ideas get built, tried and tested in the safety of a pilot, and then fall apart in the hands of the real folk who benefit from the potential of the idea. Sometimes, the idea meets with its highest criticism from those who, in fact, benefit less from its implementation. But if these groups have a disproportionate balance of power, even if they are only loosely connected to the original idea, they can close those nascent ideas down before their time. An Actor Map provides a representation that gives an overview of the service and of the context in which it will actually have to operate. In turn, as we consider where the idea may be thwarted by certain actors' understandings, misunderstandings or uses of the idea, we can use the map to inspire fresh changes to our concept, or new ideas altogether.

For example, we undertook an actor mapping exercise over a couple of hours with mixed teams from a cross-section of Japanese schools. The workshop teachers were keen to explore how they could increase the degree of student-led learning. In the context of high-stakes, high-attainment schools the notion of 'student-led learning' is very firmly a Third Horizon type goal.

The initial ideas developed by the teams in their Third Horizon work were adapted significantly, though, when they started to take into account the fact that, in the current setup of learning, the school building was the main centre of learning by far. The home and larger city of Tokyo was not used so much to inform learning, and so presented an opportunity for a good idea to become much better. Taking into account what the different actors in the wider community could offer for student-led learning, the ideas were improved with distinct actions of how parents, school visitors and Japanese higher education institutions could be put to better use as participants in student-led learning, during and outside school hours. From an idea that primarily put pressure on the schools and their teachers to make changes in teaching, the idea became something in which parents, employers and students themselves could have a clear participatory role.

The process for using this actor mapping tool is one worth having under your nose as you facilitate such a session. In terms of time, leave at least 60 minutes, and possibly a full creative session (3 hours), to leave time for the development of fresh ideas for implementation.

- Choose an innovation that you've already researched through an immersion and synthesis, ideated and maybe done a prototype or two of already, but which has not yet been publicised or socialised too much. Place it at the centre of your actor map.
- From the centre, draw a half dozen concentric circles, and split these into six slices, like a cake: WHO, WHAT, HOW, WHERE, WHEN, WHY.
- Begin filling out the WHO, from those segments that will benefit most from the idea being implemented. Think about segmenting groups beyond their larger

constituencies: e.g. engaged parents, disengaged parents, rather than just 'parents'.
- Once you've outlined all the people affected by the ideas, take each one in turn and work out WHAT they need to do to implement the idea, or what we need to do to implement the idea effectively for them, HOW this would happen, WHERE and WHEN.
- When it comes to filling out the WHY for each person, consider as much as you can from their point of view – this is a great exercise in empathetic thinking, putting yourself in their shoes. It also reveals some of the hurdles you may have to work around, changing the original idea even to make it work for these groups.
- Consider using hexagonal stickies or paper cutouts, to show how ideas connect (as we highlighted in 'Connect and cluster' Chapter 4), and don't be afraid to place certain people or actions separate from the rest, outlining the fact that they are perhaps currently disconnected, and need bringing closer to the idea at a later date.
- When you analyse the actors' map, keep a note of each action suggested by the team, as these actions will form the basis of your next idea prototype.

This process is, above all, powerful because it helps us revisit our idea not from the problem we're trying to solve or the neat ideas we've developed, but from the people we are trying to better serve. Start with the actors, the people, and consider WHY the idea is important to them.

MINI-MANIFESTOS

In 2011, my firm co-directed the digital strategy that led to the landslide re-election of the Scottish Government, the Scottish National Party (SNP), a result so strong that it redrew the political map of Scotland and led to majority approval of the country's 2014 referendum on independence from the United Kingdom. It was deemed 'the greatest achievement in modern Scottish political history' by political commentators. Some of the lessons from this campaign are pertinent to innovators anywhere as they consider how to bring people on board to their idea.

Much goes into a successful political campaign. At its core, it is built around a set of ideas to make a country better. A core dozen or so of those ideas represent the Third Horizon visions for Education, Health, Finance, and so on. In education, for example, the promise was made for 'A Smarter Scotland', with access to education based on the ability to learn, not the ability to pay. In order to make that happen, there were a multitude of other, more operational promises that made up the Second Horizon, the journey towards that Third Horizon vision of a Smarter Scotland. These included:

- Free higher education
- 25,000 apprenticeships per year
- A guarantee of learning or training for everyone up to the age of 19
- Ensuring an adequate number of teachers in relation to student numbers, and so on...

Given the complexity of running a country, these promises ran to over 39,000 words, across all sectors of Government, and came in the form of a political manifesto. A manifesto is a long document, written by one person but edited, contributed to and commented upon by many. When it is finally published in an impressive Oscars-style ceremony, relatively few voters will ever read it: its cover-to-cover audience is mostly other party members, politicians and their aides, and the press.

The parallels with a school five-year strategy are apparent: a document is prepared by a necessarily small number of people – or the Head Teacher – before being 'unveiled'. It is normally relatively plush, laid out, 'final' looking, even if the intent of the leadership team is to 'gain feedback'. The form, however, runs against the intent.

In our campaign, a plush and polished manifesto would have run against the mood of co-creation (co-creation of a new movement, a better country, together was one of the repeated words in speeches and literature). To help reduce the 'polishedness', a certain tone was communicated in subtle ways: the font used for the cover was one reflected in all campaign literature, one which looked like it had been stamped on, which showed a certain lack of polish, which showed that this was for and by the people, perhaps, open to discussion. The font was called 'Dirty'. And while most manifestos and strategy docs are normally printed on A4 or legal size paper, are thick, glossy and made highly available, on this campaign even the paper choice extended this irreverent theme. The SNP's manifesto was the size of some smaller tabloid newspapers, printed on paper that was not too thick, not too glossy.

The first challenge with such a long manifesto is that very few people, in fact, read it. First and foremost, few copies are actually printed. It is not dissimilar to a complex, lengthy school strategic plan! Not all areas are relevant to all people. Indeed, while a young family may care a great deal about access to nursery care, and want to know more about this, finding out about how the Government might invest heavily in green energy is less relevant. In fact, in some cases, if the message were to come across that spending in one area was somehow more of a priority than in the one they felt strongest about, it could be argued that such a scenario may be enough to sway them not to vote for this particular idea, and therefore for this particular party.

So, narrowing the proposition to the most meaningful components for each constituent, or customer segment, is

How To Come Up With Great Ideas and
Actually Make Them Happen

a useful exercise to undertake, to spot the merits of the idea from multiple perspectives. In our campaign work, we created the idea of the 'mini-manifesto', where we extracted the key merits from the 39,000-word manifesto and pulled together 400-800 words designed specifically for a narrow customer segment, such as young families, carers, environmental campaigners, creatives, pensioners, teachers, and so on.

There is a knack to pulling together these shorter versions of a larger idea. It is worth borrowing from the techniques of advertising copywriters. One such legendary writer, Paul Arden, had his teams frame every idea in this slightly clunky, but genius sentence, which captures most of the key points one needs to consider to overcome the bias of most folk to stay within the status quo:

This idea [give it a proper name, it makes it feel real] is the only [one of its category] that [does this] for [these people] in [this place], at a time when [What's the climate and context at the moment that makes this idea apt? Why now?]. Unlike [the competition: name them or it, even if that is 'the current way of doing things], this idea [does these things better/differently].

Such targeted messaging also permitted much more targeted communication. We knew who we wanted to appeal to most – those who had not yet decided who to vote for – and we knew from the data we had gathered over time what kinds of people they were, and what interests they had. Education institutions normally have great, but underused, data on who makes up their school community. How might the school vision be communicated in as many different ways as there are constituents in that community?

Such segmentation is key to making sure that everyone understands what it is you are trying to achieve, and that everyone sees their part in it. Trying to create one idea and communicate it in one dimension will lead to only mediocre, scattergun success. Carving the message out of each group you feel might benefit from your idea will not only help bring them on board, but begins to radically reshape those ideas to better match the people they are there to serve.

The lessons for educator innovators are numerous:

- Invest time, for sure, but find different ways to explain the same story.
- Parents have different needs to teacher peers, school leadership want to hear different things from students. Create a map of your idea for each person you want to convince to take you up on it.
- Consider putting together 'mini-manifestos' for each group, as much to get straight in your own mind what the benefits are for each group you want to buy into your idea.
- Consider how you can reduce the idea to its core information for that person.
- Work out who your idea is not for.

Although this way of explaining your idea might feel 'scrappy' or thin on detail to you, the team which has spent a considerable amount of brainpower getting things prepared, to your audiences it'll look like you've just come up with the idea, and you'll get more buy-in in the end, as people feel they can chip in with their own additional remarks, ideas and support.

PITCHING YOUR IDEA

The most formal means of sharing your idea with a leadership team, board or group of people who you would like to ask to invest their time is to pitch. Pitching is often associated with the sweat-inducing fear inspired in shows like Dragons' Den, but it should be an opportunity for a team towards the end of an ideation and prototyping sprint to really put their idea through its paces. Pitching is not just something you do if you're looking for money.

Even a not-for-profit organisation, whose goals are not to make money but to provide a service, stand to benefit from the process of preparing a pitch. Allyson Krupar, an Ohioan based in Uganda, has found the process really helped her team at the Infectious Diseases Unit in Kampala focus more on the user journey once more, something that can be forgotten as the innovator team delves deeper into the mechanics of solving any given problem: 'I was definitely thinking like an innovator but I had never thought of what I was 'selling' as a product to 'sell'.' The pitch process helps us understand whether the idea still stands up to the original problem we identified, whether it solves that problem, whether it excites people and at the same time can actually happen.

Even ideas that seem great when they've just been developed and sketched out can suffer at the point of sharing them with others if this part of your storytelling is ill-prepared. You can cover yourself with some advance preparation in the form of a pitch outline. Startups pitch to Venture Capitalists (VCs) for investment, and it's no different for a school innovator: there are both formal and informal points in your innovation journey where you have to pitch for the investment of your colleagues, parents and even students. They will be making an investment of time, energy, enthusiasm and smiles into an idea that grabs them. If your pitch fails to tempt them, they will make no investment and, without investment, all ideas run out of money and steam eventually.

We've run pitching workshops like this for both teachers, students and for entrepreneurs, across six continents. From initiation of an idea to gaining a financial investment to get the idea off the ground has taken us as few as two days, start to finish. Others have taken three months. Rarely does an idea take longer than that length of time to get investment and flourish, or have enough feedback to indicate that it's time to put it to sleep. Permanently.

We harness a template adapted from one used by MIT graduates as they pitch their services and products for investment. The innovators' goal is to end up with a ten-slide pitch, each slide lasting 30 seconds and summing up a key aspect of their product or service, the user journey, the business or sustainability case and what was going to happen next with the idea.

The very process has changed ideas, even in these late stages of developing the Second Horizon journey towards the large goal of the Third Horizon. Natasha Viau-Skreslet, one of the founders of a corruption-defeating text messaging service, describes the pain of this moment of realisation during one of our workshops: 'We came with... a prepared pitch, but it felt like on the first day that everything we had done was being dismantled and taken apart. 'We just can't fit our idea into the structure that they want!' we felt. We took it apart, and put the idea back together. The user journey crystallised where we had come from, and where we were trying to get to. It helped isolate our different users, see them each in a different way. It really helped us as a team who the beneficiaries of our platform were going to be and what exactly the service for them was going to be.'

Having been through such an extensive research and ideation phase of the First and Third Horizons, the power of thinking about how one pitches these ideas is, above all, to bring clarity. 'These ideas were vague and couldn't really transmit the information I needed to get people on board,' said Andrew Benson-Greene, a young entrepreneur from Sierra Leone whom we helped in 2011 to expand his Foundation, bringing education to neglected communities of amputees throughout the civil war-ravaged country. 'I came to realise how important these pitching steps were in order to articulate my thoughts. It's been an eye-opening experience, giving a fresh perspective to our ideas, adding brevity that was missing before and making it more likely that I'll get the support I need.'

While the idea of pitching an idea on which you've spent so much time already sounds simple, the format forces innovators to think in a different away about their original ideas, and the journey they might take towards them. Even at this late stage, the format forces reflection on whether the Third Horizon is a valid vision solving a real problem identified in the First Horizon, and whether the prototyped journey of Horizon Two is the right way forward. Key to crafting the right kind of message is thinking through who the user is, and what their user journey would look like, through storyboarding.

WHAT IS IN A PITCH?

Each point can be covered in one slide, explained in thirty seconds:

Start the pitch with a bang (and a problem)
Start with a 30-second elevator pitch which ramps up the pain of the problem you're going to try to solve. Make it grab our attention. Use the evidence from your First Horizon work to really show the problem in the real world; this is better than paraphrasing what the problem is, and people will be quicker to believe the 'pain' you are describing. This should hook us from the get-go – create intrigue, grab our attention. Don't tell us what you 'did', all the steps you went through to get this far – we're not interested in how hard you've worked! Instead, tell us what you might have discovered.

The experience
Take us on a user journey where we see the problem solved. Make sure we understand how useful this idea is in solving the problem.

The user
Who would use it? Who will it be designed to engage?
Make them real – consider showing your original personas.
Why do they want to use it?
What would they gain/ achieve?

Marketing
How will you let people know?
What will the user experience be?
What makes it unique – how will it stand out? Quantitative and qualitative value?

The benefits
Who will it benefit and how?

How To Come Up With Great Ideas and Actually Make Them Happen

What is the qualitative and quantitative value proposition?

Future
Where might it lead?

You
Convince the audience you can deliver.
Outline your previous experience.
How would this project build on your experience?

What do you want?
Do you want people's money? Time? Energy? Nod in agreement?
Where would an initial investment of $x take you, and what would you do next to take your idea further?
What would you do if there was no follow-on investment? What will you do if people's time and energy lags later into the project, and they cannot offer the time they could at the beginning? Does your idea depend on their investment of time, energy or money, or will it work to some degree even if they are not on board?
Make it clear what you are asking people to do next.

Round-up
Bring all your ideas back together again.
Why does this project have to happen?
Giving a pitch follows the same structure, every time, but the format needn't be 'stand up and PowerPoint us'. The format could be a Keynote or a PowerPoint, but it might also be a movie, Slideshare with annotations, photo story or something else. Consider how you can bring people on board well in advance by sharing your learning journey before pitching, and then think about how you can socialise your pitch after the fact with the wider school community, and earn even more support for your ideas.

NEXT STEPS IN THE SECOND HORIZON: GET YOUR IDEA OUT THERE

- ✓ Try to imbue your organisation with a prototyping culture all year around. It'll make it easier to prototype even bigger ideas in the future, when that time comes around.
- ✓ Work on feedback in everything you do: even if your school community doesn't like a new idea, can they provide kind, specific and useful feedback to contribute, rather than attempt to destroy, the innovation process?
- ✓ Make your ideas tangible as early as possible – back of the napkin explanations are better than working for weeks on a model that will get torn to shreds. People respond to ideas they don't feel you spent a lot of time on. People either hold back or provide loud, unconstructive feedback when they think you've put a lot of effort into something that won't work.
- ✓ Socialise your idea in tangible form, early and often, showing how you're listening to feedback to make it different. If people see their feedback in your evolving idea, they will continue to be part of your wider team.
- ✓ Pitch your idea formally, even if it is only for the design team to hear. Being forced to answer hard questions about how an idea will survive will help you invent additional elements that make your idea better.

MOVING FROM CONCEPT TO DELIVERY

WHEN IS A PROTOTYPE DONE?

If there were one key point to take away from our process, it is that you can never test an idea too early:

- Don't ever write a strategy and launch it 'surprise!' style to your community.
- Observe, empathise and define opportunities on what you discover, not just on what feels like a good idea or what other people are doing.
- Then, come up with as many ideas as possible, and test as many of them as is feasible.
- Use the feedback to help move your idea forward, not as something to justify your own opinions or to be ignored because it doesn't fit with what you wanted to believe.
- Test often, and test as early as you can.

This begs the question, of course: when are we actually done with prototyping and ready to say that we've got the right idea to take forward in a bigger way? When do we go from prototype to 'final version'? When can we stop soliciting feedback and just say 'we've got it!'? The simple answer is a complex one: having lived this process, you'll probably never feel quite 'done'. You will never want to stop soliciting and using feedback to tweak the idea.

The point at which a prototype becomes a 'working prototype', and enters the real world, isn't a point that one can plan for in advance. You discover you've made it when user feedback lets you know that a certain element is ready to go. The days of the 'grand launch' of a strategy of vision seem irrelevant when, if you've been undertaking a truly immersive approach like the one suggested here, nearly everyone who will make your strategy happen has contributed to its form.

Indeed, most successful innovation stories begin with a launch so soft that people barely notice it happened. The apparently endless cycle of prototype-feedback-reprototype is what leads to so many of the web services we use never losing the now-familiar 'beta' label. In fact, software developers use a staged release for their ideas, so that users have an indication of how fully baked an idea is at any given point in time:

- Alpha releases are the initial version of the prototype, where the development team know there are many issues to be fixed or created, but users are welcome to have a go and give feedback;
- Beta describes the moment where the developers think they've delivered on their key goals for the prototype, but now need more feedback to check that assumption;
- Gamma is sometimes used as another stepping stone before the final version is declared ready;
- Live describes the moment where developers' views, fed by user feedback, are that the service is ready to be declared 'done'.

Nonetheless, most developers still use data and feedback to continue tweaking even Live versions of a webpage or service, even after it has been declared 'finished'. It's become common to share what elements you'll continually seek to improve, even after launch of a live idea, on a

How To Come Up With Great Ideas and
Actually Make Them Happen

project website or on posters around your organisation.

This is what people mean when they refer to an idea or service, which appears to be quite well established, as being in 'perpetual beta'. Your strategy, too, like the scores of startups who display the term on their sites years after initial launch, will remain in a state of perpetual beta, constantly being tweaked as goals are met early, other new challenges emerge to be beaten.

When an idea feels like it's good enough to start sharing, there might still be a lack of resource – time, money, energy – to undertake all the tasks needed to make it 100% ready to put into people's lives. But you don't need a perfectly working idea to get it started. The way technology startups often make this work is to build an apparent 'full product' when, in fact, there are human beings pulling the strings to make those 'automatic emails' and 'automatic super fast signups' work. Mechanical Turks, modelled on the 'magic' fairground robot attractions that would appear to interact with real people, exist good and well in the twenty-first century.

This allows ideas to be developed fast, tweaked on the fly, without the expense of having to write expensive code. There's no point investing a ton of time and energy in making an idea ready to work for 10,000 people if you've still not had a chance to move from prototyping with 10 people to test it with 100 or 1000 people. You might put in all that effort and find that you still have more tweaking to do. It's harder to listen to feedback still when you've invested a lot in one specific direction. As Paul Graham, entrepreneur and investor, puts it:

> *Some startups could be entirely manual at first. If you can find someone with a problem that needs solving and you can solve it manually, go ahead and do that for as long as you can, and then gradually automate the bottlenecks. It would be a little frightening to be solving users' problems in a way that wasn't yet automatic, but less frightening than the far more common*

case of having something automatic that doesn't yet solve anyone's problems.

Eric Ries, in his startup bible *The Lean Startup*, repeatedly points to his own and other business failures where the majority of time, energy and finance is spent before the 'grand launch'. His first startup had worked for five years in stealth mode, spending some $40m investment with 200 employees before it launched. By the end of the product's first year in service, it had failed to capture the imagination of the mainstream public:

> *The most important mistake was that the company's 'vision was almost too concrete,' making it impossible to see that their product did not accurately represent consumer demand.*

ROME WASN'T BUILT IN A DAY – BUT 30 DAYS WOULD DO

The old saying is that 'They didn't build Rome in a day'. But people do build some huge projects in very short periods of time.

Once they've settled on the concept and the moment comes to just build it, how do they do it so fast, so well? How do they move from an idea sketched out on paper through to a beta launch of something people can use, through to the final 'live' version of their idea?

Redesigning the entire web services for a country is the kind of wicked problem that one could imagine taking years. Indeed, most Government technology programmes we equate with years of delays, overspends and dismal, out-of-date results. One team in the United Kingdom shred that image in 18 months.

If you had to redesign the website for a country, where would you start? That was the task faced by the Government Digital Service, or GDS, in the United Kingdom.

Jamie Arnold, one of the team's programme managers, was my project manager when I worked at Channel 4 Television Corporation as a Commissioner. I remember him never being without a hearty collection of 3x4' cards and a Sharpie pen.

While Jamie's filing card fetish earned him some ribbing from the rest of the team, it was an essential part of keeping us on task, and it now forms a simple but key part of the GDS's journey in rethinking how the British citizen interacts with their public services, through the web on their home computer or mobile device.

In an early set of photographs from the team's first steps to undertake this challenge, Arnold showed the same importance given over to making thinking visible as we have seen in setting the stage in the First Horizon. Underpinning the implementation of the ideas developed by Government, though, was Sprint Management. Sprint Management of a project involves defining what we want to do, why we want to do it, and how we will do it in a defined (short) period of time. It is a fundamental part of startup life, partly down to the fact that there is so little money, and so much to do, that prioritisation and pace can be the difference between a startup's life and death.

The idea is to take every task that one could undertake to build the idea, and prioritise as many as feel solvable within, say, a 30-day window: this is the 'Sprint'. The time period chosen varies. As projects advance and become more mature, they needn't stop working in sprints, although the duration of each sprint might become longer, as goals become even weightier, requiring bigger teams and management to make them happen. The latest sprint on GOV.UK, for example, has now increased to 400 working days long.

The potential tasks to be undertaken come from the Project Backlog. This Project Backlog is, in fact, the exhaustive pool of user needs or user 'pains' that need resolving, as per what we discover in the First Horizon.

The Sprint Backlog is the smaller pool of user needs or pains from the larger Project Backlog that the team feels it can solve within the existing sprint period. What's chosen for this Sprint Backlog relies upon knowing what the skills and responsibilities of each team member are: you want everyone working at the same pace, not running out of things to do halfway through, and not feeling overwhelmed and meeting failure at the end of the sprint period.

When the Sprint begins, communication is kept tight through a morning Scrum, where the entire project staff gather in a circle, standing up, for a maximum of 15 minutes. Team Leads within the staff report on what they did yesterday, what is going to happen today in order to do certain other things the day after. This means that every day, something new is being achieved. Where something crops up again, it's clear that there is perhaps a challenge that needs to be given more time, more people or some thinking put to it.

If, during the Sprint, amazing new customer insights or needs come to light, or if a new technological solution pops up, it is momentarily ignored, added to the Project Backlog to be considered at the end of the 30-day period, in the cold light of day, alongside every other competing priority. Just because something's new and shiny does not mean it's more important than the job at hand.

To help the team mark its progress, a Sprint Burndown is kept in a prominent position. At the beginning, each need is represented by a card on this Burndown. Each time a card's need has been solved, it is removed, placed on a 'Done Wall' perhaps. During the 30-day Sprint everyone can see these needs being ticked off, problems solved, ideas developed. It makes creativity and progress very visible, and maintains the pace, whether the pace needs to be kept over 30 days or 400.

LOW EFFORT, HIGH IMPACT

On a practical note, every team workshop, meeting, actor mapping exercise and pitching session will lead to a fresh set of actions for your Project Backlog. Prioritising what you do next as part of a Sprint might be easy, always based on the importance of the need as per your initial research. But if you are dealing with a large number of resources and, typically for a school, a limited daily bandwidth to achieve progress, another means might be necessary.

The two-by-four chart of effort versus impact can help

bring an analytics, pragmatic edge to your prioritisation. On the top left are items that will achieve high impact and require low effort – easy gains that will show people the best side of your ideas. As time progresses, those tasks which require more effort (and more time) can be undertaken. If items appear on that bottom right quadrant – a high effort for a low return on impact – then the team may make a decision to ditch those actions, or find an easier way to achieve the same impact.

Why is this process worth considering? Users of your idea, those outside this innovation process, will be more likely to continue playing with a fully formed small idea for some time, while more complex ideas that will make the idea bigger can be engineered in the background. The opposite – spending time, effort and money on developing something for a bigger idea before releasing it as an alpha or beta version – carries a major risk: people won't like what you've produced, and their feedback will be harder to reverse engineer into the product you've made.

A typical example at the moment in schools around the world are ideas revolving around 'maker culture', that is, the notion that students can use craft, design and technology tools to make things in order to learn. Where schools don't already have labs with craft tools, 3D printers and the like available, the first thing many want to do is spend $30,000 buying in what's required, and then setting about creating new courses that use it. Others plan and construct multi-million dollar facilities just for this type of learning. A more logical way is to look for what is easy to do but will offer a glimpse of potential impact that such a programme could have:

- Find a local Maker Space.
- Co-develop a maker curriculum with the Maker Space personnel for an after-school prototype.
- Explore if Maker Space materials can be brought to school for a Maker week.

- Try to get more permanent loan of Maker materials – a term.
- If there is impact on learning, purchase Maker materials.

DON'T THINK. TRY

After so many pages, and so many words, with so many steps on the journey, some readers might not know where to start. Well, start somewhere, but start. Now.

John Hunter was one of the Renaissance Scots who, I'd have you believe, invented the modern world. He helped set out anatomy in the terms that we understand today (before he came along people still thought the human body was made up of four gases). He believed in rigorous experimentation, lots of it and by as many people as possible, setting up his own anatomy school for that purpose.

Through this he discovered how the lymphatic system worked and undertook the first study of the growth of foetus to child. In fact, he is often associated with the first ever edition of what one might consider a medical encyclopaedia, the expensive tome all future doctors must buy on their first week of medical school. Yet, for all this experimentation and rigour, all this scientific breakthrough, his lasting epitaph is one with a far more playful timbre:

'Don't think too hard, try the experiment.'

There is a myth that if you build a great idea people will come. The problem with strategy in schools is that we don't even build a great idea – we just write it down. Ideas we build just don't attract people instantly. They need physical and intellectual effort to be made tangible, for their effects to be felt. The difference between startups that start and keep going and startups that never get started is that the founders of them, the people with the idea, work hard to recruit people to their cause. It's a manual effort. As Paul Graham, the founder of Y Combinator startup accelerator, puts it:

> *Actually startups take off because the founders make them take off. There may be a handful that just grew by themselves, but usually it takes some sort of push to get them going. A good metaphor would be the cranks that car engines had before they got electric starters. Once the engine was going, it would keep going, but there was a separate and laborious process to get it going.*
> *Bringing people to your cause in education is difficult, partly because everyone will profess to be far too busy 'doing the day job' to spend time making your next big idea work. Whether it's an extra, but great idea, or an idea contained within a school development plan, it will not happen if you don't have the users or community on your side from the very start. The leader needs to get recruiting potential users, from the very start. No more planning. Get talking and building.*

Take, for example, Principal Carolyn Cameron and some of her teachers, at Greystone Centennial Middle School, just outside Edmonton, Canada. They had a great idea during a weekend design thinking workshop in Calgary, to use this very process to rethink their annual school planning.

Most educators, frankly, would mull this issue over for some time – after all, developing a school plan is a significant task with serious consequences if it's not done 'properly', so changing the process used to form it would need to be considered at length, agreed and signed off.
So what did Cameron and colleagues do at their school? They put their idea into practice within six days. It wasn't an easy decision, but one Principal Cameron felt she had to make:

I decided it was time to walk the talk... be a risk taker, do something that was outside of my comfort zone, something that intuitively felt right.
Today, six days after participating in the Design Thinking workshop... [the] Professional Development Day was devoted to School Education planning for next year. Instead of the usual data review and collaborative work to determine what we needed to start/stop/continue in the lengthy, existing School Education Plan and Annual Education Results Report, we decided to work with staff on the Design Thinking process to create the "Best Year of My Life" for the 2014-15 school year at Greystone.

The result was hugely impactful, and provided quality feedback the First Horizon approach to things just wouldn't have brought to the surface. As a result, their school planning for the following year would be far better tailored to the needs of students, faculty and parents:

Not only was today's work engaging for our staff, but it also provided them with the opportunity to learn a process for how to be 'designers', an experience which we can work to develop with our students. It was the most engaging School Education Planning experience I have been a part of... ever! The feedback from the staff supported how I was feeling.

To put this into action has cost the school little, if any, money. But if the culture spreads to the way the teams then develop the actions from their plan, another challenge will mount: how does a school principal or bursar plan for the unplannable? How do you budget for agile development, particularly where so much of the effort in an idea is in the scoping and research side, the underbelly of an iceberg of innovation?

Back at the Government Digital Service, this is something that, four years on from the original first prototypes being produced, they have finally formalised: in fact, government departments can spend up to £750,000 ($1.5m) on research and discovery, that pre-alpha phase of development, and other controls have been built in to allow for agile development, where the end-result may not always be that clear at the beginning of a given project.

Don't think too hard about putting your nascent ideas into practice. Try, and listen to the feedback from your team, your students and your community to work out your next move. More iteration, fewer set plans, but a result that is more likely to work in the longer term.

NEXT STEPS IN MANAGING THE JOURNEY

- ✓ As you develop your idea from paper prototype to something more permanent, work out what the success criteria might look like for an alpha, beta and live version of your idea.

- ✓ Set up an implementation space, where progress on the prototype can be seen by all, and progress celebrated.

- ✓ Communicate with your team every day during the process of implementation. If that means reducing implementation to shorter sprints, do it. It's better than occasional meetings over a longer period.

- ✓ Start something. Now. Try the whole process with a smaller, non-mission-critical problem you want to solve. Gain confidence in harnessing the whole process before embarking on a tricky, wicked problem.

REFERENCES

These references appear in the order they have been cited or used in the book.

Garnett, F. (2010). Business Models v Learning Process. Retrieved from: http://heutagogicarchive.wordpress.com/2010/04/27/business-models-v-learning-process/

Quattrocchi, C. (2014, January 7). What Makes Milpitas A Model For Innovation? Edsurge.com. Retrieved from: https://www.edsurge.com/n/2014-01-07-what-makes-milpitas-a-model-for-innovation

Rosenstock, L (2012). Innovative Teaching and Learning: Lessons from High Tech High's Founding Principal. Edutopia. Retrieved from: https://www.youtube.com/watch?v=spn1xGycar8

Anthony, S. (2014, January 28). When Rising Revenue Spells Trouble. Harvard Business Review Blogs. Retrieved from: http://blogs.hbr.org/2014/01/when-rising-revenue-spells-trouble/

Zevenbergen, R. (2006). Teacher Identity from a Bourdieuian Perspective. Mathematics Education Research Group of Australasia 2006 Symposium Proceedings. Retrieved from: http://www.merga.net.au/documents/symp22006.pdf

Leadbeater, C. (2012). Innovation in Education: Lessons from Pioneers Around the World. Bloomsbury Qatar Foundation Publishing

Photographs of TEDxKidsSland, a Creative Partnerships, NoTosh Limited and Thorney Close Primary School project, by Creative Partnerships. Used with permission.

Martin, R. (2009). The Design of Business: Why Design Thinking is the Next Competitive Advantage. Harvard Business School Press

McKinsey & Company (2009, December), Enduring Ideas: The Three Horizons of Growth. Retrieved from: http://www.mckinsey.com/insights/strategy/enduring_id

eas_the_three_horizons_of_growth
Baghai, M., Coley, S., & White, D. (1999). The Alchemy of Growth, New York: Perseus Publishing.
De Bono, E. (2009). Six Thinking Hats. Penguin
Kelley, T. (2005). The Ten Faces of Innovation: IDEO's Strategies for Defeating the Devil's Advocate and Driving Creativity Throughout Your Organization.
Currency/Doubleday
Syal, R. (2013, September 18). Abandoned NHS IT system has cost £10bn so far. The Guardian. Retrieved from: http://www.theguardian.com/society/2013/sep/18/nhs-records-system-10bn
Usage and Benefits Data from Scottish Local Authorities on the use of the national schools intranet, Glow: https://wikis.glowscotland.org.uk/0000026/Glow_Availability,_Usage_and_Benefits_Wiki/Usage_Data
Chohan, A. (2011, January 25). Abdul Chohan, Essa Academy – Learning Without Frontiers, London. Retrieved from:
https://www.youtube.com/watch?v=EARTcJkNrDA
Branson, R. (2013), Like A Virgin: Secrets They Won't Teach You at Business School. Virgin Books
Hatchuel A., Le Masson P. & Weil B. (2004). C-K Theory in Practice: Lessons from Industrial Applications, 8th International Design Conference, D. Marjanovic, (Ed.), Dubrovnik, 18–21 May 2004.
Various. Leading Capital Investment Projects: Creating a vision for your capital investment project, National College for Teaching and Leadership. Retrieved from: http://www.nationalcollege.org.uk/index/leadershiplibrary/leadingschools/leading-capital-investment-projects/creating-a-vision-for-your-capital-investment-project/deep-learning-21st-century.htm
Kolko, J. (2010). Abductive Thinking and Sensemaking: The Drivers of Design Synthesis, MIT's Design Issues: Volume 26, Number 1 Winter 2010. Retrieved from: http://www.jonkolko.com/writingAbductiveThinking.php

Knapp, J. (2014, May 1). Google Ventures: Your Design Team Needs A War Room. Here's How To Set One Up. FastCoDesign.com. Retrieved from: http://www.fastcodesign.com/3028471/google-ventures-your-design-team-needs-a-war-room-heres-how-to-set-one-up

Kim, N. (2013). Discussion about learning nests / frames. Retrieved from: https://plus.google.com/u/0/105394546448464608816/posts/GU5MemjgTX1

Corney, P. J. (2014, February 1). A great knowledge capture technique: phones4u worksheet. Retrieved from: http://www.knowledgeetal.com/?p=1014

University of Stanford d.school, Method Cards for Interviewing for Empathy. Retrieved from: http://dschool.stanford.edu/wp-content/themes/dschool/method-cards/interview-for-empathy.pdf

NHS Institute for Innovation and Improvement (2008), Root Cause Analysis Using Five Whys, NHS Improving Quality. Retrieved from: http://www.institute.nhs.uk/quality_and_service_improvement_tools/quality_and_service_improvement_tools/identifying_problems_-_root_cause_analysis_using5_whys.html

Toyota Production System glossary, Toyota. Retrieved from: http://blog.toyota.co.uk/toyota-production-system-glossary

Liker, J. K. (2004), The Toyota Way: 14 Management Principles from the World's Greatest Manufacturer. McGraw-Hill Professional

Update on the CrowdED Project: https://plus.google.com/102811814098992650489/posts/hPpMYBYbY2N

Aulet, B. (2013), Disciplined Entrepreneurship: 24 Steps to a Successful Startup. John Wiley & Sons.

Richardson, C (2014). User Research: A Day In The Life.

Government Digital Service. Retrieved from: https://gds.blog.gov.uk/2014/03/07/user-research-a-day-in-the-life/

Harte, C. (2011, April). SOLO, I'm riding SOLO. Retrieved from: http://chrisharte.typepad.com/learner_evolution_chris_h/2011/04/solo-im-ridin-solo.html

Hales, E. (2013, August 23). Example of hexagonal thinking in environmental studies. Retrieved from: https://plus.google.com/114319983535204290770/posts/UCWNGeEn5Hw?cfem=1

Nguyen, A. (2013, November 27). Example of discussions around hexagonal synthesis. Retrieved from: https://plus.google.com/114662510256899461865/posts/CEZ8MMwsPse

Berger, W. (2012, September 17). The Secret Phrase Top Innovators Use, Harvard Business Review Blog Network. Retrieved from: http://blogs.hbr.org/2012/09/the-secret-phrase-top-innovato/

Lorena Sutherland (2014, February 25). It's not dumbing down, it's opening up. Retrieved from: https://gds.blog.gov.uk/2014/02/25/gds-this-week-its-not-dumbing-down-its-opening-up/

@managerspeak Twitter. Retrieved from: https://twitter.com/managerspeak/status/450934834341625856

Zander, B. Zander, B., Zander, R. (2000). The Art of Possibility: Transforming Professional and Personal Life. Harvard Business School Press.

Moore, G. A. (1998). Crossing the Chasm: Marketing and Selling Technology Products to Mainstream Customers. Capstone.

Siegel, D. (2009). Pull: The Power of the Semantic Web to Transform Your Business. Portfolio

Taleb, N. N. (2008). The Black Swan: The Impact of the Highly Improbable. Penguin.

Gray, D., Brown, S., Macanufo, J. (2010). Gamestorming:

A Playbook for Innovators, Rulebreakers, and Changemakers. O'Reilly Media

Kim, W. C., Mauborgne, R. (2005). Blue Ocean Strategy: How To Create Uncontested Market Space And Make The Competition Irrelevant. Harvard Business School Press.

Arnold, J. (2011). It's In If... photographs from project management of gov.uk project. Retrieved at: https://www.flickr.com/photos/jamie_p_arnold/6806837939/in/set-72157629142799323

Osterwalder, A., Pigneur, Y. (2010). Business Model Generation: A Handbook for Visionaries, Game Changers, and Challengers. John Wiley & Sons

Hu, W. (2011, January 5). Math That Moves, New York Times. Retrieved from: http://www.nytimes.com/2011/01/05/education/05tablets.html

Grannell, C (2010, December 30). The School That Gives Every Student an iPad. Techradar. Retrieved from: http://www.techradar.com/news/computing/apple/the-school-that-gives-every-student-an-ipad-915539

We Launched A New Service That Gives You A New Way To Talk To Your Local Police Force, Snook. Retrieved from: http://wearesnook.com/snook/?case=mypolice

Various authors, Portugal's Magellan Initiative: Preparing the children for a knowledge-based world. Retrieved from: http://en.wikibooks.org/wiki/One-to-One_Laptop_Schools/Portugal

Leicester, G., Bloomer, K., Stewart, D., Ewing, J. (2013). Transformative Innovation in Education: a Playbook for Pragmatic Visionaries. Triarchy Press

Goodwin, B. (2011, February) Research says... One-to-one Laptop Programmes Are No Silver Bullet, ASCD. Retrieved from: http://www.ascd.org/publications/educational_leadership/feb11/vol68/num05/One-to-One_Laptop_Programs_Are_No_Silver_Bullet.aspx

Berger, R. (2003) An Ethic of Excellence: Building a

Culture of Craftsmanship with Students, Heinemann Educational Books.
Watch How Google X Employees Deal With Failure, FastCompany. Retrieved from: http://www.fastcompany.com/3029114/most-innovative-companies/watch-how-google-x-employees-deal-with-failure
Gertner, J. (2014) The truth about Google X: An exclusive look behind the secretive lab's closed doors. FastCompany. Retrieved from: http://www.fastcompany.com/3028156/united-states-of-innovation/the-google-x-factor#1
Gebbia, J. (2013) Joe Gebbia: Executing Your Idea Starts With a Single Step, 99U Conference Video. Retrieved from: http://vimeo.com/77144446 See 07'55"
Hulme, T. (2011, August 2) It's OK to launch before you're ready. Financial Times. Retrieved from: http://www.ft.com/cms/s/0/85f988e8-bd4c-11e0-89fb-00144feabdc0.html#ixzz2zuujYZmz
Maker's Alphabet on Kickstarter. Retrieved from: https://www.kickstarter.com/projects/makersalphabet/makers-alphabet
Graham, P. (2013) Do Things That Don't Scale. Retrieved from: http://paulgraham.com/ds.html
Business Model Canvas tool. Retrieved from: http://www.businessmodelgeneration.com/canvas
Otabil, B. (2011) ITU Young Innovators on Pitching. NoTosh Publishing. Retrieved from:
 https://www.youtube.com/watch?v=hWSu54AblZs
Lamarre, D. (2008, November 25) Daniel Lamarre of Cirque du Soleil. Video by INSEAD. Retrieved from: https://www.youtube.com/watch?v=iinPELvQHm0
Cirque du Soleil Mission and Goals. Retrieved from: https://www.cirquedusoleil.com/en/jobs/recruitment/life/progression.aspx
Farrell, M. P. (2003) Collaborative Circles: Friendship Dynamics and Creative Work. University of Chicago Press.

Torrance, D. (2012, January) A Winning Formula. Total Politics Magazine. Retrieved from: http://www.totalpolitics.com/print/281837/a-winning-formula.thtml

Arden, P. (2003) It's Not How Good You Are, It's How Good You Want To Be. Phaidon Press.

Krupar, A. (2011) Allyson Krupar ITU Young Innovator. Video. NoTosh Publishing. Retrieved from: https://www.youtube.com/watch?v=NHDwgLXXTts

Viau-Skreslet, N. (2011) Natasha Viau-Skreslet ITU Young Innovator. Video. NoTosh Publishing. Retrieved from: https://www.youtube.com/watch?v=mpZKZ4xHwAE

Scott, T. (2014) A Year in The Making: The Digital By Default Service Standard. Government Digital Service. Retrieved from: https://gds.blog.gov.uk/2014/04/01/a-year-in-the-making-the-digital-by-default-service-standard/

Ries, E. (2011) The Lean Startup: How Today's Entrepreneurs Use Continuous Innovation to Create Radically Successful Businesses. Excerpt retrieved from Wikipedia: http://en.wikipedia.org/wiki/Lean_Startup

Sprint14 on GOV.UK: https://gds.blog.gov.uk/category/digital-engagement/sprint-13-2/

Cameron, C (2014) Walking the walk: teachers as designers. Retrieved from: http://www.psdblogs.ca/greystone/2014/05/16/walking-the-talk-teachers-as-designers/

Wilks, D. (2014) Getting Approval for Agile Spending. Government Digital Service. Retrieved from: https://gds.blog.gov.uk/2014/04/11/getting-approval-for-agile-spending/

James Hunter image. By John Jackson (died 1831), after Sir Joshua Reynolds (died 1792) [Public domain], via Wikimedia Commons